Foil Fencing

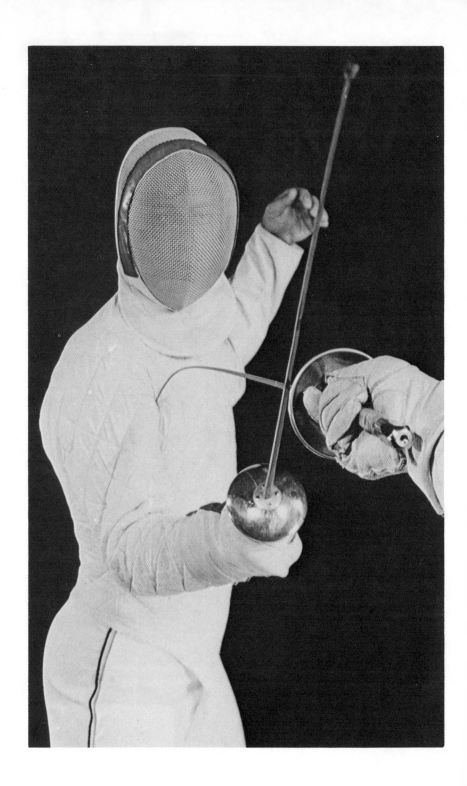

Foil
Fencing

Skills, Safety, Operations,
and Responsibilities for the 1980s

Maxwell R. Garret
and
Mary Heinecke Poulson

with a discussion of legal responsibility
by Steve Sobel

The Pennsylvania State University Press
University Park and London

Library of Congress Cataloging in Publication Data

Garret, Maxwell R
    Foil fencing.

    Includes glossary and index of fencing terms.
    1. Fencing.   I. Poulson, Mary Heinecke,
1930–   joint author.   II. Sobel, Steve,
joint author.   III. Title.
GV1147.G37   796.8'6   80-18426
ISBN 0-271-00273-5
ISBN 0-271-00274-3 (pbk.)

Printed in the United States of America

Contents

Foreword

This book is a valuable addition to the growing body of United States literature on the sport of fencing. While fencing is one of the most rewarding sports for the participant, it is also one of the least known in the United States. This book will help to disseminate basic knowledge of the game to all interested persons.

Fencing is practiced formally in about seventy countries that hold active memberships in the International Fencing Federation (F.I.E.). The heartland of the fencing world has always been the continent of Europe; the countries of the Americas and of Asia and Africa generally follow the lead of the Europeans in the development of the sport. The current trend toward popularization of this ancient and aristocratic game among all segments of society in the United States was foreshadowed by earlier and similar movements in France, Italy, and Hungary following the First World War, and by the strong impetus given to fencing as a "people's sport" on a national scale in the Soviet Union and other socialist countries after the Second World War.

Fencing is both old and new. Its infinite variety gives it the capacity of periodic rejuvenation with the changing times. At the turn of the twentieth century the dominant interest of fencers centered upon the endless combinations and permutations of attack and defense with the weapon that makes fencing so similar to chess. Although child prodigies were not unknown, preeminence in the sport belonged to adults. Today there is a worldwide movement toward simplification of the game, particularly at the competitive level, by concentrating upon a limited number of basic actions with the weapon, perfectly executed, and upon the athletic fundamentals—mobility, timing, speed, and endurance. Modern technology has accelerated the process through the invention of electrical judging of touches. This is a game for young people, and young competitors are coming to the fore in fencing as they have done generally in other sports.

Professors Garret and Poulson have combined their talent and experience as fencing teachers with their expertise in the broader field of physical education. They have chosen to limit their technical instruction to the one weapon that is used by both men and women in competition, leaving to others the development of similar guides to the épée and the saber. However, the make-up of the book reveals that they have made an interesting and shrewd judgment about the pleasures of fencing. There is no real equivalent in this sport to the week-end golfer or tennis player. Some form of organized competition generally provides the greatest satisfaction, even for the fencer who does not aspire to national or international recognition. Therefore, informative chapters have been included on judging and the organization of fencing tournaments, which require the active participation of fencers at all levels of skill.

I would like to add a few words of special praise for the sections on safety and legal responsibility—topics that are of enormous importance to fencers, coaches, administrators, and anyone else seriously interested in the development of the sport on a healthy national basis.

I congratulate the authors and publishers of this book.

Miguel de Capriles
Former President, Fédération
Internationale d'Escrime.

Preface

The main purpose of this book is to introduce the novice fencer to the game of fencing. It is also intended to achieve the following:

Share the fun and excitement of fencing with anyone interested.

Satisfy a layman's curiosity regarding the sport of fencing.

Help the instructor/coach organize lesson plans.

Complement and supplement the fencing instructor's lessons.

Assist the experienced fencer in developing the total game.

Inform and guide fencers, coaches, officials, and administrators regarding safety and legal responsibilities in fencing.

The scope is comprehensive but not exhaustive. This book offers an approach to fencing in which subject matter is structured around concepts. When specifics are forgotten, an understanding of the concept will enable a fencer to recall and apply information more easily. Learning experiences built around these concepts help the fencer learn by doing. These learning experiences and the highlights at the end of each chapter can be easily adapted to fencing lessons.

The authors are grateful to Stephen Sobel, counsel and past president of the Amateur Fencers League of America, for contributing Chapter 14, "Liability and Negligence."

The authors are deeply indebted: to Professor Miguel A. de Capriles for the Foreword; to Russell Johnson for acting as sounding board and critic, and for his analytical comments and suggestions; to Diana Garret for many reasons, especially for giving her time to listen, and for keeping us nourished during our work sessions; to Esther Garret Beimfohr for her artistic services; to Rosa Lee Brill, Linda Woodring, and Peg Krumrine for their proficient typing and patience; to David Shelly and Phyllis Dolich for their professional photographic work; to Bart Fried for his line drawings; to the Amateur Fencers League of America for permission to reprint a synopsis of their visual aids and fencing rules; to the National Fencing Coaches Association of America for permission to use excerpts from the NFCAA Manual; to The Athletic Institute, Arthur Schankin, and Anthony Zombolas for permission to use several of their photographs; to Miguel A. de Capriles and Stanley G. Sieja, co-authors with Maxwell R. Garret, for their permission to use material from their *Tournament Guide;* to Penn State fencers John Corona, Mitchell Dorfman, Jim Ellis, Jeff Haney, Matt Harris, Steve Kaplan, Donald Lear, Cathy McClelland, Judy Smith, Ben Way, and Joseph Zagorski for their pictorial contributions. Most especially the authors commend the staff of The Pennsylvania State University Press.

Above all, the authors hope the enjoyment and excitement they have found in fencing will be transferred to each reader.

M. R. G.

M. H. P.

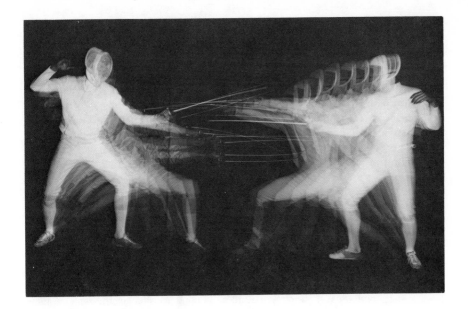

1

The Attraction of Fencing

Concept: Fencing, a Fine, Combative Sport, Provides Lifetime Opportunities for Participation and Creative Expression.

Cyrano De Bergerac—D'Artagnan—The Three Musketeers. Who has not dreamed of walking side by side with these swordsmen, confident of his ability to handle any situation and to be master of his own fate? This need not be an idle dream. Learning to fence is within anyone's grasp.

Modern fencing provides many opportunities for participation.

Fencing is a year-round sport with many attractive attributes: it can be conducted either indoors or outdoors on a nonskid surface; boys and girls as well as men and women may enjoy the sport; people of any age, body build, or temperament can experience success; a fencing practice area may be as small as a living room or as large as all outdoors. Many high schools, colleges, voluntary and public agencies, and private clubs provide facilities and fencing instruction not only throughout the United States but also throughout the world. From their interest and participation in fencing, many people have developed hobbies collecting weapons, books, old fencing manuscripts, dueling prints, and art objects pertaining to the sport.

Opportunities for fencing competition are almost endless. There are local and divisional tournaments open to anyone interested. Sectional, national, and international tournaments are conducted for those who qualify from the local and divisional events. The Junior Olympic fencing program provides age groupings for Under-16 and Under-20 and sponsors an annual national championship from which are selected fencers to represent the United States at the Junior World Championships. Some tournaments are for novices, some for teams, some for couples, and some for individuals. The ultimate in fencing competition is to be selected to represent one's country in the Olympics, in the Pan American Games, in the World Fencing Championships, in the World University Games, or in the Junior World Championships.

People are attracted to fencing for many reasons.

Once their interest is captured, people pursue fencing for the same reasons they pursue such activities as singing, painting, playing musical instruments, solving mathematics problems, piloting airplanes, or playing basketball. These activities satisfy their need to use their abilities and thereby become significant, creative, and personalized beings.

LEARNING EXPERIENCE—ATTRACTIONS OF FENCING

Why are you attracted to fencing? When you think of fencing, what images come to mind?

Many lessons of life can be learned on the fencing strip.

The satisfaction of hard work.
The importance of exercise for total fitness.
The development of self-confidence.
The ability to take defeat and bounce back to victory.
The realization that failure is merely a detour to success.
The acquisition of discipline.
The channeling of the unspent part of aggression into higher emotional attitudes.
The embracing of opportunities to reduce tensions and increase satisfactions.
The confrontation of many problem situations and the determination of solutions.

Paul Gallico, who started fencing at age thirty-seven, referred to fencing as follows:

> [It is the] release trigger for the outpouring of personality, temperament and self. It is an old axiom of fencing that five minutes on a strip behind a weapon, and a fencer has revealed himself, his nature, his character, his honesty, his mental capacities—his very essence. As you are, so you will fence. You can

conceal nothing, nor can your opponent. Your inner selves will clash upon the strip as sharply as your steel—there is no royal road, no easy shortcut to the joys of combat fencing. The price is . . . hard work and discipline, of sometimes tedious practice routines. But the rewards thereof are great and satisfying. Once the drudgery has been put behind, the fun comes fast and furious and never ending.[1]

LEARNING EXPERIENCE—LESSONS OF LIFE

Take special note of the lessons of life that can be learned in fencing. When you have entered your first competition after acquiring the basic skills, check the list again to see what lessons you have learned on the strip.

Three weapons are used in the sport of fencing—the foil, the saber, and the épée.

While the target area and the style of fencing differ among the weapons, there are similarities in technique and timing. Most fencers begin their training in foil and branch out into saber and épée. Some fencers concentrate on developing proficiency in one weapon, others become proficient in two weapons, and some in three. Since many skills learned in foil generally apply to saber and épée, *this book will deal solely with foil fencing* so a beginner can develop one coherent skill and not be burdened initially with the nuances of the three weapons. Hereafter, in this book, "fencing" refers to foil fencing only.

Differences among Foil, Epée, Saber

Weapon	Target	Method of Scoring	Description	Original Use of Weapon
Foil	Torso	With tip only	Thin, tapered quadrangular blade. Small bell guard.	Training
Epée	Entire body	With tip only	Thick, tapered triangular blade. Large, heavy bell guard.	Dueling
Saber	Everything above hips	With tip *and* cutting edge	Y- or T-shaped blade. Large, crescent-shaped bell guard.	Cavalry

---

[1]Aldo Nadi, *On Fencing* (New York: G. P. Putnam's Sons, 1943), p. xv.

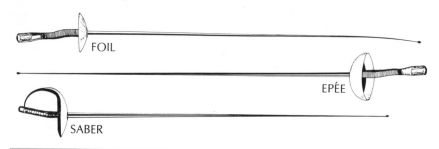

FOIL

EPÉE

SABER

LEARNING EXPERIENCE—FOIL, EPÉE, SABER

1. *Ask a fencer to show you the three basic weapons and to explain their similarities and differences.*
2. *Observe competition in foil, épée, and saber, noting especially the similarities in technique and timing and the differences in target areas and styles.*

Foil fencing is a combative sport, the object of which is to hit the opponent with the point of the weapon on the trunk of the body.

The valid target includes the trunk of the body from the collar to the groin in front and, on the back, to a horizontal line passing across the top of the hip bones—that is, the area outlined by a regulation jacket minus the arms. The arms, legs, mask, and the bib of the mask are invalid target areas. Theoretically, a valid hit (that is, a hit within the prescribed target area with the point of the weapon) might be fatal. Any graze or slap with the weapon is not considered a valid hit. A fencer hit on an invalid target such as the arms, legs, or mask, would theoretically be wounded, but not fatally.

VALID TARGET: FOIL

A fencing bout is conducted on a rectangular mat (strip, piste) having the layout and dimensions shown in the diagram. A fencer wins a bout by scoring five valid

DIAGRAM OF FENCING STRIP
(foot-and-inch dimensions are not
exact equivalents)

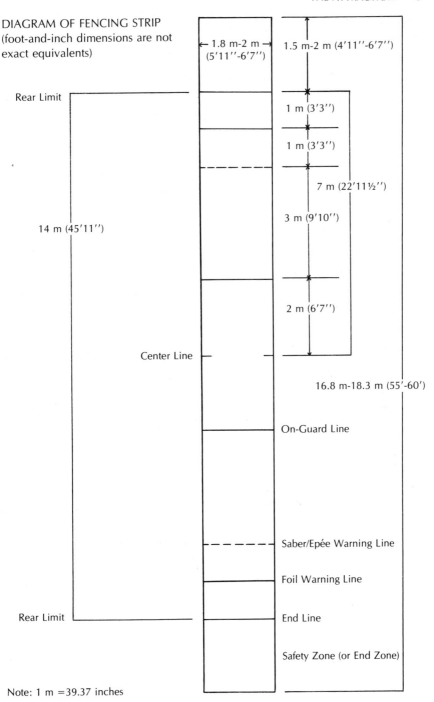

Rear Limit

← 1.8 m-2 m →
(5'11''-6'7'')

1.5 m-2 m (4'11''-6'7'')

1 m (3'3'')

1 m (3'3'')

7 m (22'11½'')

3 m (9'10'')

14 m (45'11'')

2 m (6'7'')

Center Line

16.8 m-18.3 m (55'-60')

On-Guard Line

Saber/Epée Warning Line

Foil Warning Line

Rear Limit

End Line

Safety Zone (or End Zone)

Note: 1 m =39.37 inches

hits or touches upon the opponent. The time limit for scoring the touches is six minutes of actual fencing time.

Fencing promotes physical, emotional, and mental growth.

Fencers are dependent upon their ability, ingenuity, comprehension, judgment, and skill—with no assistance from outside sources. Unlike some team games, no substitute player or special play can be sent into the bout. The sport does not depend upon a specific body type.

Many competitions are held on round-robin schedules and it is not unusual for a fencer in a national tournament to fence 15 to 25 bouts in a day. This schedule places a premium on endurance in addition to the requirements of skill, agility, balance, quickness, power, and good coordination.

To cross blades with an opponent requires courage. Even though the weapons are blunted and flexible and even though all safety precautions have been taken, a beginner may feel shyness and reluctance to be touched by a weapon. But courage can be developed and instilled. The development of courage can be of great psychological value to the fencer by enhancing self-confidence and the ability to make decisions under stress.

LEARNING EXPERIENCE—OBSERVING A BOUT

Observe a fencing bout (match). What did you find difficult to understand? What elements of the game were easy to understand? Were the actions difficult to follow? Did you observe one fencer, both fencers, or the blade action? Did you comprehend the interpretations of the officials?

HIGHLIGHTS
1. Explain why fencing is considered a lifetime sport.
2. List several lessons of life that can be learned on the fencing strip.
3. Explain the similarities and differences among the three fencing weapons.
4. Point out the boundaries of the valid target.
5. Describe the differences between a valid and an invalid hit.
6. Identify and name the main areas on a fencing strip.
7. State the time limit and the number of hits required for winning a bout.
8. List several physical, mental, and emotional values to be gained from fencing.

2

The Fencer's Gear

Concept: Foil, Gloves, Jacket, Mask, Trousers, and Gym Shoes and Socks Are Basic Equipment Needed to Participate in Fencing.

Knowing how to select, care for, and maintain the equipment is imperative.

The foil is a thrusting weapon composed of blade, bell guard, pad, handle, and pommel.

A new foil will arrive assembled unless otherwise requested.

The blade is four-sided and tapers to a blunted tip. The pommel is attached to the threaded end of the blade. The foible of the blade is that part near the tip which is thinnest and weakest. The area closest to the bell guard is the strong part or the forte.

By rule, a blade may be no longer than 90 cm (about 35.4 inches). Blades may vary in length up to this limit. While a shorter blade does not reach as far, some feel that it has less whip and can therefore be better controlled.

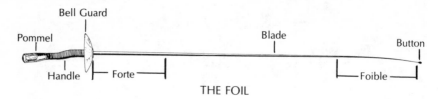

THE FOIL

Blades are currently manufactured in France, Spain, Italy, England, the U.S.S.R., Hungary, and Japan. Consult experienced fencers to determine what brand of blade is the most durable and will give the best service. X-raying blades can uncover weak spots in the steel.

New blades are very straight even though flexible. It is essential that a new foil blade be bent so the point deviates downward. This bend will increase blade life by causing it always to bend in the same direction. The bending of the blade insures the safety of a fencer by absorbing the force of the impact when the blade touches the target.

LEARNING EXPERIENCE—BENDING THE BLADE

1. *Examine several used blades. Are they bent properly? Why should they be?*
2. *There is a definite method to be used in maintaining the proper bend of the blade. Hold the foil with the handle close to the floor and slide the sole of the foot along the foible of the blade until a slight downward curve or bend has been set along the forward part of the blade. An experienced fencer or teacher may demonstrate how to bend the blade properly.*

Although the tip of the blade is blunted, it is nevertheless steel and requires additional padding by wrapping adhesive tape around the blunted end (button).

The blade is the only part of the foil that occasionally needs to be replaced. With care, the remaining parts will give many years of service. Extra blades and rubber or plastic tips should be ordered when purchasing a foil.

The bell guard, made from either steel or aluminum, is a concave circular plate to protect the hand and arm from the opponent's point. It is lined with a pad of leather or felt that cushions the fingers. Should a blade or bell guard show signs of slivering, use a file to remove the rough edges. Remove rust with fine sandpaper.

The handle (hilt or grip) is made of wood, plastic, or metal. It may be covered with leather stripping, heavy cord, plastic twine, or insulating material.

Three basic handle shapes were developed from the French, Italian, and Spanish schools of fencing. The French school, using a straight handle, stressed fingerplay with the thumb and forefinger serving as manipulators of the blade, and the other three fingers used as aids.

The Italians added a cross-piece to the bell guard. The thumb and forefinger gripped the flattened portion (ricasso) of the blade; the middle finger passed through the outer ring between the guard and cross-piece; the other two fingers were placed on the handle which was bound to the wrist by a strap. These factors enabled the fencer to use strong, forceful movements. The Italian school empha-

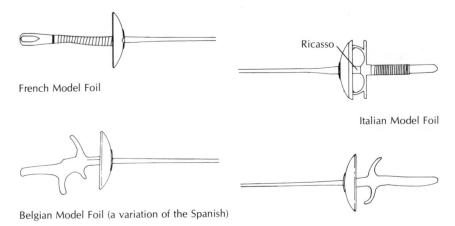

French Model Foil

Ricasso

Italian Model Foil

Belgian Model Foil (a variation of the Spanish)

Spanish Model Foil

BASIC HANDLE SHAPES

sized an on-guard position with the blade almost horizontal and the foil arm almost fully extended.

Handles gripped as a pistol are classified as orthopedic types. They received their inspiration from the Spanish schools. It is felt that they enable the fencer to use both strength and fingerplay to the best advantage.

Most fencing teachers in the United States recommend that a beginner use a foil with the French handle. It is the least expensive and is widely used. More importantly, many instructors feel that beginners can best learn the nuances of fingerplay with this handle.

The pommel is a metal counterweight that secures the handle, bell guard, and blade. Many pommels have a hole at the end into which an eye-screw can be inserted for suspending the foil when it is not in use or for attaching a martingale.

The martingale is a thin loop fashioned of leather or string inserted between the handle and bell guard. When wrapped around the fingers or wrist, it prevents the fencer from dropping the foil when disarmed.

A glove with padding and gauntlet is essential to protect the fencer from injury.

The glove is usually made of suede or other leather and is sometimes reinforced at points that wear out most readily. However, any glove with gauntlet (a padded cuff which extends over the sleeve of the jacket) is suitable if it prevents the opponent's foil from entering the sleeve of the fencer's jacket.

To prevent the glove from being hardened by perspiration, let it dry at normal room temperature after it has been used. To aid the drying process, insert absorbent material into the glove. For shape retention a replica of a hand inside the glove is useful. A few drops of neatsfoot oil will keep the glove soft and pliable. To extend the life of a glove, reinforce those areas where the handle comes in contact with the glove.

A safe fencing jacket provides sufficient protection and padding.

The fencing jacket fits snugly but not too tightly. According to the rules of the Amateur Fencers League of America, all women's jackets must have extra protection in the bust area. In addition, the wearing of a plastron (a padded garment with one sleeve) is obligatory for both men and women to insure added protection of the target area. Since the groin area is a valid target, it is recommended that a jacket with a cuissard (groin strap) be worn.

Jacket closings may be buttons, zippers, or self-adherent material. Jackets that button or self-adhere have the open edge away from the foil arm.

Repair any holes or worn spots immediately. Jackets should be washed often. To avoid shrinkage, follow the manufacturer's instructions, or wash in lukewarm water, rinse, and always hang up to dry. Since bleach tends to weaken the cloth fibers, it should be used sparingly if at all. A loose-fitting jacket offers a larger target; therefore, select a jacket that is form-fitting but still allows freedom of movement. A cotton T-shirt worn underneath the jacket will absorb perspiration as well as give added protection.

Any person whose hair touches the jacket needs to pin it up so it cannot be entwined in a foil or invalidate a touch made on the lamé vest.

Safety considerations require a mask to be well constructed and free of dents, and to fit the head snugly; the bib should cover the neck area.

Heavy mesh wiring soldered together for reinforcement is used in the construction of a mask. When dented, the mesh is weakened. Should denting occur, the mask should be repaired and refurbished. Some manufacturers provide this service. Masks with rusted mesh are dangerous and should be discarded. A Zivkovic mask with a lucite face shield has been recently developed and has been approved by the FIE.

Masks can be purchased in different sizes and can be adjusted for safety and comfort. They may be trimmed with canvas, plastic, or leather. The bib of the mask must be heavy white quilted cloth or plastic, and should be cleaned frequently.

Trousers or slacks are necessary to protect the legs.

Many fencers wear sweat pants during fencing practice. The important factor is that the legs be covered. Shorts are definitely unsuitable and unsafe. Knickers and knee socks are commonly worn for competitions.

Shoes must have rubber soles to provide traction and comfort.

Never fence in shoes with hard leather soles, in bare feet, or in stocking feet.

Certain guidelines should be used when selecting fencing equipment.

Consult a fencing teacher, ask the advice of experienced fencers, or write to the authors of this book.

Order equipment early, either through an institution or a sporting goods store, to insure prompt delivery and to allow sufficient time for making adjustments or exchanging equipment. Allow sufficient time for delivery. All personal equipment should be marked for identification.

Be properly fitted. The materials used for trousers and jackets should be sanforized or preshrunk to insure proper fit. Shoes and socks must be fitted well to avoid blisters and other foot discomforts. Masks should fit snugly. If eyeglasses are worn, masks should accommodate the glasses without creating an uncomfortable feeling for the fencer.

Purchase high-quality equipment. The mask, jacket, and glove are necessary protective gear. Do not sacrifice safety by purchasing inferior equipment.

Order from reputable sources known to provide good service and high quality products. A good representative listing of suppliers of fencing equipment may be found in the magazines *American Fencing* and *The Swordmaster.*

Keep informed of rule changes affecting equipment requirements. Arrange with fencing manufacturers and dealers to receive their latest equipment catalogs. Note changes in design, materials, and protective features.

LEARNING EXPERIENCE—EQUIPMENT COMPARISON

Examine several designs of fencing equipment. Compare quality, style, and prices. Which equipment is best for you? Discuss equipment needs with your instructor/ coach or an experienced fencer.

HIGHLIGHTS

1. Identify the parts of a foil.
2. State the advantage of the short blade and longer blade.
3. Explain why a new foil blade should be bent, in what direction, and how it should be done.
4. Describe the tip of the blade and how it should be covered.
5. Explain the purpose of the bell guard.
6. Identify the three basic handle shapes and explain.
7. Explain why the French-style handle is recommended for beginners.
8. State the functions of the pommel and the martingale.
9. State the functions of the glove and how it should be cared for.
10. List three criteria for determining a good jacket.
11. Describe a good mask.
12. State the functions of trousers and rubber-soled shoes.
13. List four guidelines for equipment selection.

3

Basic Skills

Concept: Mastering Basic Skills Is a Prerequisite to Efficient Performance.

Skills should be learned in a logical and progressive sequence. The time required to develop each skill will depend on the abilities, attitudes, goals, background, and motivation of both you and your teacher.

When each new skill is learned, it should be combined with previously learned skills so you will later be able to use the skill in the context of a bout and not become merely a storehouse of isolated skills.

A written explanation and discussion of fundamental skills cannot convey the excitement and vitality of fencing. It is a dynamic and mobile sport. Therefore, after reading this section, the authors suggest that the reader observe experienced fencers in a competition or in a film to note how all the parts of each movement are related and combined into a continuous action. Such observations will give added meaning to the fundamental skills that will now be discussed.

The ability to hold the foil correctly is the key to good offensive maneuvers.

As was mentioned in Chapter 2, there are three basic designs for fencing handles—French, Italian, and Spanish (at times called orthopedic or pistol). This text will refer only to the French-design handle.

The handle of the French foil is shaped and curved to rest comfortably in the hand. Place the second phalanx of the index finger on the underside of the handle close to the bell guard and place the thumb flat on the topside of the handle just above the index finger. The handle now rests against the palm of the hand just beneath the fleshy part of the thumb. Close the remaining three fingers lightly but firmly around the other surface of the handle. The thumb and index finger are called the *manipulators*. They move the point in any direction with a minimum amount of assistance from the wrist and preferably with none from the arm and shoulder. The three remaining fingers (called *aids*) are used to control the movement of the blade.

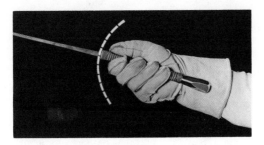

THE GRIP

LEARNING EXPERIENCE—GRIP AND FINGERPLAY

1. *Compare a right-handed and a left-handed French foil.*
2. *Grip the foil with only the manipulators. Using only the thumb and index finger, trace the following shapes with the point of the foil:*

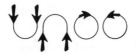

3. *Use a door knob as a point of reference and draw shapes around it using the three aids to control the movement of the blade.*
4. *Hold the foil by its tip and try to lift it using only your fingertips.*

The position of attention is preparatory to the salute and on-guard positions.

In the sequence of commands given runners, such as "On your mark! Get set! Go!" the "On your mark" position is similar to the attention position in fencing. It is a preparatory position that fencers assume as they salute their opponents with the foils and don their masks.

Stand erect with the feet at right angles. The heel of the rear[1] foot is placed against the side of the leading foot near the heel so that the imaginary right-angle lines drawn will coincide with the inside and outside edges of the rear foot and of the leading foot as shown in the diagram in the Learning Experience that follows. The rear arm is extended alongside the body with the palm against the thigh. The weapon arm is extended with palm up and with the foil directed at the opponent's feet. The body is relaxed with the leading shoulder directed at the opponent.

LEARNING EXPERIENCE—ATTENTION

Mark two lines at right angles with chalk or tape. Assume the position of attention. Are your feet placed as shown in the diagram?

LEADING FOOT

In fencing, the salute is a symbol of good will and sportsmanship dating back to the days of dueling and chivalry.

A brisk, swashbuckling movement of the sword once denoted that a combatant recognized his opponent as worthy and was prepared to defend himself within the rules of the duel.

Today, however, the salute is brief and brisk, but remains a symbol of courtesy and sportsmanship. Many variations of the salute are used at competitions. The salute described below is simple and to the point:

THE SALUTE

[1]For a right-handed fencer, "rear" refers to the left foot, leg, shoulder, arm, or hand; "leading" refers to the right.

(a) Stand at attention. Hold the mask with the rear hand. Grip the foil. Extend the weapon arm and foil diagonally toward the opponent's feet.
(b) Raise the extended arm and foil until they are parallel to the floor with the tip of the foil directed at the opponent. Flex the elbow, bringing the guard close to the lips, with the tip of the foil pointing upward.
(c) With a brisk movement, extend the weapon arm toward the opponent.
(d) Don the mask and be ready for combat.

The on-guard position is the basic stance for all fencers.

The expression "on-guard" implies that the fencer is ready mentally and physically for any action. The position enables the fencer to be mobile, it provides the maximum reach, and it limits the amount of valid target area presented to the opponent. The position has been likened to sitting on the edge of a chair. Since it requires the use of muscles ordinarily not called upon to support the body, a fencer

ON-GUARD

may experience initial discomfort until his muscles have been properly conditioned.

The on-guard position requires four steps which are gradually combined into one continuous movement: step out, sit down, lift rear arm, lift leading arm.

The "step out" is executed by moving the leading foot forward so the feet are approximately shoulder-width apart.   Keep the weight equally distributed between both feet.

The "sit down" is executed by flexing both knees with the leading knee over the instep of the leading foot and the rear knee over the rear foot.   Sit down as if on the edge of a chair or desk, keeping the body erect and the hips in line as though a plumb line had been dropped from the top of the head to the floor. The center of gravity is now lowered, giving the body greater stability and mobility. Body weight should be equally and centrally distributed.

LEARNING EXPERIENCE—ON-GUARD, BODY BALANCE

To determine whether or not the body is in a perfectly balanced position, lift one foot off the ground, the lift coming from the hips, and put it back on the ground quickly. This should be followed with the same rapid movement by the other foot. The arms are held straight out from the shoulders to form a straight line from fingertip to fingertip. If your arms appear to rock as your feet are alternately and quickly lifted and put down, the weight of your body is poorly distributed; otherwise, the weight is probably well centered.

The rear arm is lifted and flexed to form a right angle.   Raise the rear arm away from the opponent forming a continuous straight line with the shoulders. Flex the elbow; flex the wrist, keeping the fingers together and pointing them toward the opponent; relax the hand. This arm position serves several purposes: it counterbalances the position of the foil arm; it prevents the arm from drifting in front of the target area; and it reduces the amount of valid target area facing the opponent.

LEARNING EXPERIENCE—ON-GUARD, REAR ARM

Is your rear arm in the correct and most effective position? Apply this test. With the rear arm in the position described above, move it gradually away from your opponent, thereby offering less target to him—but, stop moving the arm when it reaches a point where it causes the leading knee to move from its perpendicular position over the leading foot.

The leading arm is flexed, the weapon threatening the opponent.   With foil arm extended toward the opponent's feet, with palm up, raise the arm to shoulder height. Consider the bell guard as the face of a clock. The weapon and hand should be in supination—that is, fingers and palm at 12 o'clock and the thumb at 3 o'clock. The foil pommel and handle rest on top of the wrist. This hand position helps prevent the elbow from drifting to the outside of the body.

Flex the elbow but not the wrist, maintaining a straight line from the weapon hand to the elbow. Flex the elbow until the hand is breast-high and the elbow is approximately 6 inches from the body—ahead of and below the leading shoulder.

The foil should be an extension of the forearm with the pommel positioned above the wrist. To raise or lower the point, flex the arm at the elbow. Do not flex the wrist.

The fencer should keep the head erect, looking directly at the opponent, to maintain good vision and balance. The point of the weapon should be at the fencer's own eye level or slightly lower.

The foil arm, positioned between the two opponents, will act as a shield. The elbow should not protrude outside the body. Such a position would expose more of the valid target, reduce the strength of defensive capability, and minimize point control.

LEARNING EXPERIENCE—ON-GUARD POSITION

1. *Using a full-length mirror, look at your image as you assume the on-guard position, and imagine it to be an opponent. Assume a hand position which does not expose to your "opponent" any target area on the outside of the blade. This will be your initial on-guard hand position.*
2. *Using a full-length mirror, assume the on-guard position. Is your on-guard similar to the illustration on page 15?*

Proper footwork is essential for mobility in fencing.

A mobile fencer is difficult to hit, launching attacks quickly and moving out of range readily. In fencing, movement is either forward or backward (advancing or retreating). With a moving target the attacker must constantly adjust distance, timing, and speed to create the opportunity for a possible score.

The distance covered by an advance or retreat will differ with each situation.

THE ADVANCE   THE RETREAT

Through training, observation, and experience, a fencer will learn to regulate the distance according to an opponent's style and technique.

An advance or forward step is used to close the distance between fencers. To execute the advance, lift the toe of the leading foot and step forward approximately one foot length, placing the heel down first. As the ball of the leading foot is set down, the rear foot should be brought forward the same distance covered by the leading foot. The advance can be executed in a two-count cadence: step forward with the leading foot, landing on the heel; then bring up the rear foot and simultaneously set down the ball of the leading foot. For greater mobility, skim rather than drag the feet.

A fencer uses the retreat or the step back to avoid being hit, to maintain distance, or to lure the opponent toward him. Extend the rear leg, placing the ball of the rear foot approximately one foot length behind the original position. Bring the leading foot back an equal distance, placing the entire sole of the foot firmly on the floor.

LEARNING EXPERIENCE—ADVANCE AND RETREAT

1. *Imagine the ceiling of the fencing room as only a trifle higher than the height of your body in its on-guard position. As you practice the advance and retreat, avoid lifting your body upward or bobbing (causing your head to hit the imaginary ceiling). You will then move in a horizontal line without wasted effort.*
2. *Vary the distance of the advances and retreats.*
3. *Can you combine the advance and retreat into various patterns such as advance-retreat, retreat-advance, advance-advance-retreat?*
4. *How quickly can you execute double advances and/or double retreats—that is, two rapid advances and/or two rapid retreats?*
5. *Vary the speed of your advance and retreat drills by responding to an established cadence.*
6. *After executing several advances and retreats, check the distance between your feet to make certain the base of support is the same throughout.*
7. *Close your eyes and listen as you advance and retreat. Are the sounds you hear crisp and decisive or shuffling and slow?*

The extension of the weapon arm is necessary to threaten the opponent by moving the point toward the target.

To score in foil fencing a fencer must hit the opponent with the tip of the foil. To do this, extend the arm and aim at a specific spot on the target. The extension of the weapon arm threatens the opponent, forcing him to defend himself.

With the weapon arm in the on-guard position, extend the arm, raising the hand to shoulder height and keeping the hand supinated. The pommel of the foil will lie close to and above the wrist. Because hand movements must be made with split-second timing, it is absolutely essential that the extension be a relaxed, smooth, lightning-fast movement. *Be careful not to lock the elbow through hyperextension*

EXTENSION (THRUST)

nor to elevate or hunch the shoulders. As the extension is being completed, slightly flex the wrist, permitting the point of the weapon to descend toward the target. To recover from the extension, flex the elbow and return it to its original position.

LEARNING EXPERIENCE—ARM EXTENSION

1. *Combine the extension with the advance and the retreat: extend, advance, retreat, on-guard.*
2. *Advance with the extension. As the extension begins, advance.*
3. *Repeat the same with the retreat until the movements are smooth, controlled, and rapid.*
4. *To aid in point control, try to pin a dropped glove against a wall mat by extending the foil arm. Have a fencing partner release a glove against the wall from varying heights above the fencer's head. (The "drop the glove" game can be adapted to many skills for developing reflexes and point control.)*

The lunge is an aggressive action designed to enable the fencer to reach the opponent from a distance greater than that afforded by extension of the weapon arm.

To reach the opponent, first extend the foil arm. Then propel the body forward by stepping out with the leading foot. Acquire added momentum by vigorously extending the rear leg while keeping the rear foot as stationary as possible.

The component movements of the lunge should be blended into a smooth, flowing, continuous action, beginning with the leading arm, then the leading leg, rear leg, and rear arm.

The leading (foil) arm initiates the attack.   The extension of the leading arm as already discussed is one of the most significant skills to be mastered. Movement of the leading foot prior to the extension of the foil arm will telegraph the attack. Start

THE LUNGE

(1)

(2)

(3)

(4)

(5)

(6)

the attack by extending the foil arm shoulder high, quickly stepping forward with the leading leg.

The leading leg takes an exaggerated walking step forward. When stepping forward, raise the toes slightly and extend the leg, keeping the knee at the same elevation while skimming the heel across the fencing mat. (Land on the heel before setting down the ball of the foot.) At the completion of the lunge, the lower leg is perpendicular to the floor with the knee over the instep. If the angle formed at the knee is less than 90 degrees, a fencer has not lunged to the maximum. At the conclusion of the lunge, the feet are still at right angles as in the on-guard position. The length of the lunge will vary with the distance between the fencers.

LEARNING EXPERIENCE—EXTENDING THE LEADING LEG

To acquire the skill of extending your leading leg, place a glove across the instep of your foot. Lifting the toes and extending the leg will propel the glove sharply forward and slightly upward.

The rear leg provides the force that propels the body toward the opponent. As the heel of the leading foot skims the floor, vigorously extend the rear leg, driving the body forward. The rear leg in the lunge can be compared to a coiled spring under compression which, when released, imparts energy and force.

The rear foot is the source of power and the point from which the lunging distance is measured. It is important that the foot remain flat and firm to maintain the desired distance.

The rear arm is extended away from the opponent. To counteract the forward momentum of the body, extend the rear arm smartly to the rear, parallel to the fencing mat, palm up. Any major change from the normal pattern of extending the rear arm will cause the point of the foil to deviate.

LEARNING EXPERIENCE—THE LUNGE

1. *Using a mirror or a fellow fencer as a critic, practice extending your rear arm back to a point parallel to the floor and then parallel to your rear leg. Compare the effect of each method on the movement of your foil arm and the tip of your weapon.*
2. *Conduct the same comparison, but this time extend the arm to the right and left sides and then directly back. How do these variations affect your foil arm and the tip of your weapon?*
3. *Try lunging by coordinating all of the following four actions into one flowing movement:*
   a. *Extend leading arm.*
   b. *Extend leading leg, landing on heel of leading foot.*
   c. *Extend rear leg and keep rear foot flat and firm.*
   d. *Extend rear arm backward parallel to the floor.*
4. *Practice ten lunges and hold the position after each lunge. Check and correct*

the position of each body part. Remember to keep your body weight equally distributed on both legs and your body erect. How do you feel? Uncomfortable? Muscles straining? If the lunge is executed as described, you will be uncomfortable. The physical demands of the lunge are severe, but the musculature can adapt to the demands if you use appropriate conditioning measures.

The return or recovery to the guard position is made either to the rear with the rear leg remaining stationary, or forward with the leading leg stationary.

The fencer should not remain in the lunge position, hence must be prepared to recover quickly. To recover to the rear from a lunge, flex the rear knee first. Push off with the heel of the leading foot and return to the *original* on-guard position. Return the rear arm, then the foil arm to their original positions.

To recover forward from a lunge, flex the rear knee, bring the rear leg forward, and return to the on-guard position, keeping the body low. Flex the rear arm and return it to the on-guard position. The leading arm remains extended or returns to the on-guard position, depending on the opponent's reaction.

LEARNING EXPERIENCE—LUNGE, RECOVERY, AND FOOTWORK

1. Practice five lunges with immediate recovery to the rear.
2. Practice five lunges with immediate recovery forward.
3. Combine all the footwork learned thus far into sequential drills such as advance, retreat, extend, lunge, recover forward; double retreat, extend, advance, lunge, recover to the rear.
4. Practice advancing, retreating, lunging, and recovering on two balance beams, 4 to 6 inches in height, placed parallel to each other.
5. Vary the tempo at which the combinations are executed, trying to increase the speed gradually while still retaining efficient form.
6. Holding the foil, practice various drills employing the retreat, advance, lunge, and recovery. Ask the following questions while practicing:
    a. Is the tip motionless?
    b. Do the weapon, the hand, and the forearm form a straight line from the tip of the elbow to the tip of the blade?
    c. Is the tip of the foil at eye level?
    d. Is the wrist firm and straight?
    e. Is the thumb at three o'clock?
    f. Is the elbow of the leading arm in the proper position?

Four quadrants or lines—called high, low, outside, inside—are formed by two imaginary lines intersecting at the bell guard.

The four lines or areas are used to learn the relationship between the blade, the hand, and the target, and to understand defensive positions with regard to the target. When the foil is held in a central guard position and the thumb is at three o'clock, the *high line* is the area above the bell guard; the *low line* is below the bell guard. The *outside line* is the area adjacent to the thumb; the *inside line* is the opposite area, thus establishing four areas of reference: *outside high line, outside low line, inside high line,* and *inside low line.* The areas are so designated in relation to the fencer's bell guard, not to the target. It is conceivable, therefore, that the four areas vary as the blade is moved.

It is impossible to protect the entire target area at one time. For example, when protecting (or closing) the outside high line, the other three areas are unprotected (or open). Likewise, if the inside high line is protected or closed, the inside low, outside high, and outside low lines are unprotected or open and therefore subject to attack.

Outside High Line 6

Outside Low Line 8

Inside High Line 4

Inside Low Line 7

FENCING LINES AND TARGET AREAS

In order to protect a specific area, the hand and foil are placed in certain positions numbered 1 through 8 for purposes of identification.

Protection Positions

Position	Hand	Point of Blade	Protects
1. Prime	Pronated	Below bell	Inside high
2. Seconde	Pronated	Below bell	Outside low
3. Tierce	Pronated	Above bell	Outside high
4. Quarte	Supinated	Above bell	Inside high
5. Quinte	Pronated	Above bell	Inside high
6. Sixte	Supinated	Above bell	Outside high
7. Septime	Supinated	Below bell	Inside low
8. Octave	Supinated	Below bell	Outside low

The hand may be supinated (palm up) or pronated (palm down); the blade correspondingly may be above the hand or below. The chart of Protection Positions illustrates which of the eight positions protects each area. In fencing, the emphasis is on mobility and simple movements. Of the eight positions, only four are commonly used: 4, 6, 7, and 8. Prime (1), seconde (2), tierce (3), and quinte (5) are used less frequently.

A beginning fencer, by becoming familiar with just two positions (4 and 6), will be able to develop a basic defense. These are also the positions most frequently used by fencers of the highest skill level.

Hand Position for 6. Weapon hand should be in a position with thumb at three o'clock and blade covering (protecting) the outside high line.

Hand Position for 4. Weapon hand should be in a position with thumb at three o'clock and blade covering (protecting) the inside high line.

There are slight variations in the hand and blade positions as taught by some instructors. Some advocate various degrees of pronation (turning palm down) of the hand as the fencer moves from 6 to 4. The authors suggest that the hand remain supinated (palm up) when moving from 4 to 6 and from 6 to 4 for two reasons: (1) to maintain point and blade control; and (2) to keep the tip of the weapon closer to the target area.

LEARNING EXPERIENCE—HAND POSITIONS 4 AND 6

Stand in front of a mirror. The image you see will be similar to that of an opponent facing you.
1. *On-guard.*
2. *Move to position 6 (cover the 6 line). Look into the mirror at your "opponent." If any part of the target area is visible in the outside high line, the position is not correct and the 6 line is not covered and protected from an attack.*
3. *Now do the same with position 4.*

Caution: *Avoid exaggerated lateral movements from 6 to 4 and 4 to 6 that resemble a windshield wiper.*

Contact of the blades is called engagement.

The purpose of engaging an opponent's blade is to determine by touch where the blade is and how it is being held—loosely or tightly. (*Note:* The opposite of engagement of blades in which there is no blade contact is called absence of blades or absence of blade contact.)

Blades are engaged according to fencing lines. For example, an engagement of 6 means that the blades are crossed in 6—that is, the fencers, if they are both right-handed or both left-handed, have their 6 line protected with the blades on the outside of one another. Each fencer in this case has the 4 line open. An engagement of 4 is the reverse. Therefore, if both fencers are engaged in 6 and either one extends and/or lunges, the valid target should be covered.

The most common engagement is that of 6 since most fencers feel more confident about defending their 4 line.

The disengagement (from 4 to 6 or 6 to 4) is a simple attack from a closed to open line made by lowering the point on one side and lifting it to the other.

This indirect attack moves from the line of engagement into another line in one continuous, fluid motion. It is the most frequently used attack and its mastery is essential for success in fencing.

The disengagement requires finger control. The last three fingers (the aids), if released or relaxed from the grip of the foil, will cause the blade point to descend. When the three fingers resume their original grip, the point will ascend. Lowering the point on one side and lifting the point on the other side is accomplished by alternately relaxing and tightening the grip without lateral movement of the arm. The most effective point movement is in the shape of a narrow U that keeps the point constantly on target, rather than a broad or circular U that causes the point to move on and off the target.

Executing the disengagement is comparable to inserting a light bulb into a socket. The bulb is moving both forward and in a circle. In a disengagement the point is continually moving forward even as it descends on the one side and ascends on the other. The hand remains supinated.

LEARNING EXPERIENCE[2]—DISENGAGEMENT

1. *Engage in 6—Disengage from 6 to 4 with a bent arm so that concentration is on finger movement.*
2. *Engage in 6—Disengage from 6 to 4, extending the arm as the point drops and rises. The bell guard should move directly toward the target.*
3. *On-guard in 6—Maintain absence of blade contact. As your opponent moves his foil laterally from 4 to 6, disengage. Disengage before he contacts your blade. This maneuver is called evading your opponent's blade as he tries to contact your blade and is the beginning of learning the art of deception, so vital to the enjoyment and success of fencing.*
4. *Repeat the same sequence with the 4 position.*

The change of engagement (engaging in a new line) and double change of engagement (to a new line and back) add variety to a fencer's repertoire.

Change of engagement (from 4 to 6 or 6 to 4): This is executed by passing the point *under* the opposing blade (in a manner similar to that of the disengage) and moving the hand into the line of opposition. Such a movement brings the point into the opponent's open line while still holding the opponent's blade. This skill enables a fencer to move quickly from one line to another, keeping the opponent in doubt as to what the next move will be. The development of a more extensive repertoire of movements makes the fencer less predictable and more difficult to defeat.

---

[2]The Learning Experiences in this concept and all others in this book are for two right-handed or two left-handed fencers.

LEARNING EXPERIENCE—CHANGE OF ENGAGEMENT

1. Engage in 6.
   a. Change the engagement and move the hand into 4.
   b. Advance with the change of engagement so the change and the advance are completed simultaneously.
   c. Retreat with the change of engagement.
   d. Advance with the change of engagement, extend, and lunge.
2. Engage in 4 and repeat.

Double change of engagement: This is doubly effective and consists of changing from one line to another and then back to the original line. The first change is a crisp action; the second, a holding or sustained action similar to the single change.

LEARNING EXPERIENCE—DOUBLE CHANGE OF ENGAGEMENT

1. Repeat number 1 of the change of engagement learning experience, doing a double change instead of a single.
2. Engage in 6. Add mobility to the double change. Advance and double change. The leading foot moves with the first change of engagement (beat); the rear foot with the second change of engagement (hold).

Parries block attacks by deflecting the opponent's blade.

Lateral parry: A fencer can defend with a lateral parry by moving the blade laterally across the body. Only after successfully parrying the attack may a fencer initiate an attack. The rule of right of way favors this sequence. The theory behind it is simple. If fencers used lethal weapons, it would be suicidal to attack when being attacked.

The lateral high-line parries 4 and 6 can be executed either by (1) a crisp, percussive beat to bounce the opponent's blade away, or (2) moving the hand as

PARRY 4   PARRY 6

well as the blade in order to block the opponent's threat and at the same time to maintain blade contact.

Parry 4 is used to defend against an attack coming into the 4 line. The hand is supinated and moves just far enough in the direction away from the thumb to close the line. (It is important to think of a parry as a means of closing the line to the attack. It would be folly to reach for the opponent's blade if it were not threatening the target.) A fencer should parry as though building a sturdy wall for protection against an onslaught. This should help avoid excessive flexing of the wrist. The parry needs the force of forearm, wrist, and blade. The entire forearm moves in a direction away from the thumb, with the point moving slightly farther than the hand.

Parry 6 is used to defend against an attack into the 6 line. The action requires coordinated movement of the supinated hand and forearm pivoting from the elbow. The blade closes the 6 line by contacting the opponent's blade with a sustained action. All learning experiences for parry 4 can be used for learning parry 6.

Circular parry: This describes a near circle (down and around) picking up the opponent's blade and carrying it back to the original line of engagement. Instead of initiating the action, the circular parry responds to an attack and deflects the attacking blade.

CIRCULAR 4 PARRY   CIRCULAR 6 PARRY

Circular 6 parry is executed in a clockwise direction for right-handed fencers; circular 4 parry is executed in a counterclockwise fashion for right-handed fencers. The effect is a "digging" one (down and under). The circular movement is made in relation to the opponent's blade; that is, if the attack is high, the defender will not have to dig as much as if the blade were lower. Because of the distance the point travels in executing this parry, it requires a longer time to execute but will protect a larger area.

A riposte is a counterattack executed immediately after a successful parry.

As soon as a fencer parries, an attack should be initiated immediately. An attack immediately following a parry is a riposte and gives a fencer the right of way. The key word is *immediately*. A parry that is held without a riposte may enable the opponent to persist in attacking. (See Chapter 4 for an explanation of *right of way*.)

LEARNING EXPERIENCE—PARRY AND RIPOSTE

Reciprocal exercises in which each person has a specified role provide the basis for learning fencing techniques. Neither fencer should make a bout out of an exercise. Each fencing movement has a rhythm. Only when a novice feels the rhythm of a movement should an attempt be made to execute it more rapidly.

THE RIPOSTE

1. *On-guard in 6.*
   Fencer A—Extend in 4 and lunge, remaining in the lunge.
   Fencer B—Parry 4.
2. *On-guard in 6.*
   Fencer A—Extend in 4 and lunge, remaining in the lunge.
   Fencer B—Parry 4 and riposte with extension of blade arm.
3. *On-guard in 6.*
   Fencer A—Extend in 4, lunge, and recover.
   Fencer B—Parry 4, extend, and lunge with simple, direct riposte.
4. *On-guard in 6.*
   Fencer A—Advance with the extension in 4, lunge.
   Fencer B—Retreat parrying 4, extend, and lunge with simple, direct riposte.
5. *Engage in 6.*
   a. *Fencer A—Disengage.*
      Fencer B—Circular parry 6.
   b. *Fencer A—Disengage, lunge.*
      Fencer B—Circular parry 6, extend.
   c. *Fencer A—Disengage, lunge, recover.*
      Fencer B—Circular parry 6, extend, lunge.
6. *Practice the above also from the on-guard and engagement in 4.*
7. *Add mobility to the drill by retreating as you parry.*
8. *Use the disengage to help your partner respond with a circular parry.*

A feint is a mock attack toward one area with intention to strike another portion of the target.

In boxing, a feint to the belly may culminate in a blow to the head. In fencing, a feint may be executed with any portion of the body as in other sports, but feints are usually made with the foil, to draw a reaction or a parry.

Any extension of the blade can be a feint. If the opponent responds with either a lateral or circular motion, a fencer can deceive the attempt to parry. To deceive the opponent, move the foil point with the fingers. The bell guard, arm, and hand should never change position but continue to move forward giving the impression of a straight attack.

The feint must appear to be a sincere attack (therefore, made with an extending or extended arm) or the opponent may not respond. A fencer should deceive the opponent's blade, *as the opponent starts to react, not after the opponent has reacted.* This split-second timing is possible because the fencer has predetermined what the opponent's reaction will be.

LEARNING EXPERIENCE—FEINTS

1. *Practice a full extension (a feint) with vigor to help create a threatening situation. The opponent responds to the attacker's feint. The attacker deceives the opponent's blade.*
2. *On-guard in 6 (also practice in 4).*
   Fencer A—Extend into 4 (extend into 6).
   Fencer B—Parry lateral 4 (parry lateral 6).
   Fencer A—Deceive with a disengage lunge.
   (This maneuver is called the feint of a straight thrust followed by a disengage.)
3. *On-guard in 6 (also practice in 4).*
   Fencer A—Extend into 4 (extend into 6).
   Fencer B—Attempt a circular 6 parry (circular 4 parry).
   Fencer A—Deceive, following the direction of the opponent's blade, and lunge.
4. *To learn to execute a feint, first make a simple attack with a lunge against a stationary opponent. Practice the same attack with an advance instead of a lunge. This is a proper feint. Watch yourself in a mirror and see if you can make your feint resemble a real attack.*

The beat, change beat, glide, and pressure are actions against an opponent's blade that prepare the way for an attack.

Beat attack: This is a sharp, crisp action made with the middle of the blade against the weak part of the opponent's blade for the purpose of deflecting the opponent's blade. This attack is particularly successful against a fencer who consistently has the foil arm extended.

To execute the beat, relax the last three fingers or aids and then contract them with a *very slight* wrist and forearm action. The contact with the opponent's blade should be decisive. At the moment of contact, the point of the blade is still approximately "eye high" so that an extension of the weapon will bring the point to the target.

LEARNING EXPERIENCE—BEAT

The progression used in learning the beat can be applied to learning all attacks. On-guard in 6:
Beat against another blade to get the feeling.
Beat and extend against another blade.
Beat and extend against an extended blade.
Beat, extend, and lunge.
Advance and beat, extend, lunge.
Retreat and beat, extend, lunge.

All attacks can be made toward all lines. For example, a beat attack, directed at an unprotected 4 line, would be called a *beat 4*.

A beat 6 can be executed against a blade directed toward an unprotected 6 line.

The beat 6 is executed in a slightly different manner from the beat 4. The beat 6 employs greater forearm action, pivoting from the elbow which remains fixed. At the conclusion of the beat, the pommel should be parallel to the forearm and lying close to the wrist. The movement is directed toward the outside line.

Each hand movement can be used as an attack or as a parry—as an offensive movement or as a defensive movement. The beat 4 and beat 6 have been discussed in terms of attacks against the blade rigidly held by the opponent. The same movement can be used as a parry or means of defense against an attack, or as an aid to establish a cadence.

Change beat: This is a combination of the disengage and the beat, executed with the arm bent. It is executed in the same manner as the first change in the double change of engagement—that is, by relaxing the last three fingers, moving the point to a new line, and firmly gripping the handle to beat the blade crisply. The fencer can follow this action with a straight thrust.

LEARNING EXPERIENCE—CHANGE BEAT

1. Engage in 6 (also practice 4).
   a. Change beat.
   b. Change beat, extend.
   c. Change beat, extend, lunge.
2. Engage in 6 (also practice 4).
   a. Add mobility by advancing (or retreating) with the change beat and extension. The synchronized actions should be as follows: leading foot moves as change beat is executed; rear foot moves as extension is executed; lunge.

Glide (coulé): This is the taking of the opponent's blade, maintaining momentary contact and control. The weapon arm is extended in the line of its engagement, maintaining contact with the opponent's blade by gliding along it. The glide should maintain control and leverage over the blade, and should be brief and quick. It can be executed with or without opposition (taking the blade without releasing it).

Other terms used rather interchangeably with the glide are coulé, graze, and froissement, each differing slightly from the others but all of them basically involving the same principle—that of maintaining contact with the blade while gliding straight toward the target.

Pressure: This is a sustained action against the opponent's blade rather than the percussive action of the beat. The opponent's blade can be deflected by pressing it aside. Imagine a cat crouching until the moment it springs. This movement is similar to the pressure attack in which a fencer presses the foible of the opponent's blade, maintains the pressure until he senses the tactile reaction, and then springs to the target. Start the leading foot just slightly before releasing the opponent's blade to add decisiveness to the attack. If the opponent reacts by pressing in return, follow the preparatory action with a disengage.

The purpose of these preparatory movements is to elicit a reaction from the opponent. A fencer must be prepared to deal with that reaction.

(a) If the opponent resists the pressure or the glide or reacts to the beat, deceive the movement with a disengage.
(b) If the opponent yields to the pressure or glide, execute a circular movement to deceive the blade.
(c) If the opponent does not respond at all, go straight to target.

A victim of a preparatory movement must be prepared to defend against it.

(a) Do not maintain an extended arm position unless inviting the opponent to act against the blade.
(b) Evade the blade as the opponent initiates the action.
(c) A counter preparatory movement can be successful against an opponent whose preparatory movements are indecisive. For example, your adversary presses against the blade; a quick counter pressure attack may take the adversary by surprise.

Attacks are either simple or compound aggressive actions intended to score against the opponent. (Compound actions are covered in Chapter 5.) The simple attacks may be direct or indirect.

A *simple direct attack* is an action into the line of engagement while a *simple indirect attack* is an action into the opposite line of engagement. Both actions involve a single blade movement.

Straight thrust: The straight thrust is the only simple direct attack and may be used with or without a lunge. Its execution has been covered but it is important to emphasize that speed, proper timing, and accuracy are essential for its success. Constant practice is necessary to coordinate the extension of the weapon arm with the lunge. This attack must be executed with precision without telegraphing one's intention.

LEARNING EXPERIENCE—SIMPLE DIRECT ATTACKS

1. Engage blades.
   Fencer A—Move blade to opposite line.
   Fencer B—Straight thrust and lunge.
2. Engage blades.
   Fencer A—Extend weapon arm as though intending to attack. Return instead to
     the original position.
   Fencer B—Straight thrust and lunge as Fencer A begins the return to the original
     position.
3. Absence of blade contact.
   Fencer A—Has high guard position.
   Fencer B—Straight thrust and lunge into lower target area.

Simple indirect attacks: These include the disengagement and the cutover. The
execution of the disengagement has been described. The size of the disengagement
is determined by the path the point must take around the opponent's bell guard and
by the distance to the target.

LEARNING EXPERIENCE—DISENGAGEMENT

Engage blades in 6 (4).
Fencer A—Start to change engagement.
Fencer B—As the change begins, start disengagement, deceiving your opponent's
  attempt to engage blades, extend, and lunge.

The cutover (from 4 to 6 or 6 to 4) is an inverted disengagement. Instead of
passing beneath the opponent's hand, the cutover passes over the tip of the opponent's weapon, ending in the opposite line of the engagement. As the weapon arm
is drawn back slightly, the forearm is raised partially with a slight flexing of the
wrist. As soon as the tip of the opponent's blade is cleared, extend the forearm
smartly down and forward, threatening the target on the other side of the blade.
The entire action must be swift and decisive. Indecision or faulty execution may
provide the opponent an opportunity to counterattack.

LEARNING EXPERIENCE—CUTOVER

1. Engage blades.
   Fencer A—Press the opponent's blade.
   Fencer B—Cut over, extend, and lunge.
2. Engage blades.
   Fencer A—Start to change engagement.
   Fencer B—Cut over, extend, and lunge.

The *fencing distance* is the physical relationship between two adversaries. *Fencing measure* is usually defined as the maximum lunging distance required to reach the target, and differs for each fencer.

Since fencers differ in height, in flexibility, and in arm and leg length, sense of distance becomes a very important skill in competition. The ability to gain or break (change) the distance requires excellent footwork and a precise evaluation of one's own distance to attack. This is the method a fencer uses to get within reach or out of reach of the opponent.

Distance is the interval separating two fencers, and is maintained by advancing (gaining ground) or retreating (yielding ground). In fencing, four distances have to be considered:

1. Short distance, which is riposting distance.
2. Middle distance, which is lunging or attacking distance (also known as the *measure*).
3. Long distance, which is the distance for flèche attack or for attack that requires a forward movement, i.e., advance and balestra, before the attack.
4. Infighting distance, which is closer than riposting distance.

The *measure* (French *la mesure*) is the distance at which a fencer may touch the opponent with a lunge attack.

Timing complements fencing distance and is the ability to seize an opportunity to attack the opponent at the right moment.

Choosing the right moment to act is important because every offensive action can be defended, *if* the defender has sufficient reaction time or a sense of time. Speed is important and necessary, but unless you can adjust your timing to that of your opponent, speed can be wasted and result in an uncontrolled, poorly timed, and ineffective action. (See Chapter 6 dealing with strategy.)

HIGHLIGHTS

1. Demonstrate the proper way to grip a French foil and how to manipulate the point.
2. Holding the mask and foil, assume a position of attention and execute a brisk salute. Explain the purpose of the salute.
3. Describe the four steps of the on-guard position. Explain why a fencer assumes this basic stance.
4. Describe the two steps in executing the advance and demonstrate a series of three advances. Do the same for the retreat.
5. Demonstrate how to extend the weapon arm and recover.
6. Demonstrate a good lunge with recovery forward and recovery to the rear.
7. State in how many positions the hand and foil may be placed to protect the target. Demonstrate which are the most basic positions for the beginner.
8. Demonstrate a disengagement from 6 to 4 and explain how it is accomplished with the fingers.

9. Execute a double change of engagement from 6 to 4 and back while engaged with another fencer.
10. With another fencer executing a lunge in 4 and 6, execute the appropriate circular and lateral parry.
11. Define riposte and state its function.
12. State the purpose of the feint and the main feature to consider in its execution.
13. Against an opponent, execute each of the preparations in number 6, above.
14. List three ways to counter these preparatory movements.
15. Differentiate between the simple *direct* and *indirect* attack.
16. Differentiate between the disengage and the cutover.
17. Define fencing measure and state two ways of maintaining it.
18. Explain the importance of timing.

4

Rules of Competition

Concept: Fencing Competitions Are Governed by Rules Designed to Insure Equity and Safety for Each Fencer.

The rules of fencing outline the framework for the application of skills and knowledge; they are presented in condensed form in this chapter. Many rules are incorporated into other chapters of this book as indicated in parentheses. The unabridged rules and regulations governing conventional and electric foil fencing are listed in the current edition of the *Amateur Fencers League of America Fencing Rules*. The *Fencing Guide* of the National Association for Girls and Women in Sport also includes the rules and interpretations. (Today's rules for foil fencing are basically the same as those adopted in 1914 in Paris. The rules concerned with electrical apparatus and equipment were adopted in 1957.)

"Ignorance is no excuse," according to the official rules; therefore, each fencer should, through study and competition, become familiar with the rules.

A fencing bout is held on a piste of regulation size.

The piste (strip or mat) measures between 1.8 meters (5 feet 11 inches) and 2 meters (6 feet 7 inches) in width. Its length is 14 meters (45 feet 11 inches). End zones or safety zones extend beyond each end of the strip proper by 1.5 to 2 meters (4 feet 11 inches to 6 feet 7 inches), making the total length 17 to 18 meters (55 feet 9 inches to 59 feet).

A fencer is required to bout within the boundaries of the strip. (See Chapters 1 and 6.) Certain conventions govern crossing the end and side boundaries.

If a fencer retreats to the warning line, which is 1 meter from the end of the strip, the president will halt the bout and warn the fencer. Should the fencer gain ground to the original on-guard line and then return to the 1-meter line, the bout is halted again and the fencer is advised of his predicament. If the rear boundary line is crossed with both feet, a touch is scored against the fencer who crosses it.

When a fencer crosses the lateral (side) boundary of the strip with one foot, the president halts the bout, ordering him *on-guard* at the point where he crossed the lateral boundary line. No penalty is imposed. When a fencer crosses with both feet, the opponent is instructed to move forward 1 meter.

A fencing bout is under the control of the president assisted by four judges, a scorekeeper, and a timekeeper. (See Chapter 7.)

The president decides the validity or priority of a hit; the judges determine the materiality of a hit. In electric foil fencing, the electric scoring device replaces the four judges. The scorekeeper and timekeeper assist the president.

Before a bout begins, the scorekeeper announces the names of the opponents according to a prescribed order as explained in Chapter 7. The fencer whose name is called first by the scorekeeper stands behind the guard line to the right of the president except when the first-called is left-handed and the opponent is right-handed.

The president gives the order "On guard," then asks "Ready?" If the fencers respond affirmatively, or in absence of a negative reply, the president orders "Play!" or "Fence!" Then the bout officially begins. The fencers continue bouting until the president calls "Halt!" Play is resumed in the middle of the strip after a touch is scored, and at the same place where it is halted if no touch is scored. When using nonelectric foils, fencers change sides after one fencer has received half the maximum number of hits, that is, three. In electric foil fencing, fencers do not change sides.

The immediate goal of bouting is to score legal hits (touches). (See Chapters 1, 6, and 7.)

A hit is scored when the point of the weapon arrives on a valid target—that is, the trunk of the body including the groin area plus the collar area in the front, and the collar to the hip joints in the rear. The bib of the mask is not a part of the target.

A fundamental rule as to scoring hits is the rule of *right of way*. It is employed by the president in determining the validity and priority of a hit when both fencers are hit at approximately the same instant. Generally speaking, the rule states that a fencer initiating an aggressive action in which the weapon is moving forward, threatening the opponent, has the right of way *until* the opponent defends and counterattacks. Then the opponent has the right of way. If the opponent fails to parry and initiate an attack, or after parrying hesitates before counterattacking, the original attacker is able to resume the attack and thus maintain the right of way. When the two fencers are hit at the end of the same phrase, if there is a great difference in time, only the first hit scores. But if the difference is small, the hit having the right of way is scored even if it arrives after the other hit. If the two hits arrive about the same time and neither has the right of way, no touch is scored.

The winner of a bout is the person who first scores five hits within a set time limit. (See Chapters 1 and 7.)

The duration of a bout may vary in accordance with conference rules. However, in official AFLA competitions, bouts comprise six minutes of actual fencing time (the time between the orders "Fence" and "Halt").

When the time limit expires before the bout has been completed, the following apply:

(a) If one fencer has received more hits than the opponent has, the number of hits required must be added to the score to bring it up to five, and the same number of hits must be added to the opponent's score.

(b) If both fencers have received the same number of hits, they are both regarded as having received the maximum number of hits being fought for, less one, and they fence for the last hit without time limit.

Differing methods and styles may be employed providing the fencers adhere to the rules and conduct themselves safely and courteously.

Infractions of the rules and conduct of fencing carry penalties that range from loss of ground on the strip, as incurred when crossing the strip boundaries, to expulsion from the competition, as might occur in certain cases of unsportsmanlike conduct.

A book of this length cannot possibly include all offenses and penalties. Before entering a competition, a fencer should know what constitutes an offense and the penalties that accompany each offense. The official rules manual provides such information in detail.

Common courtesy and common sense will indicate the conduct expected whether drilling, practicing, bouting, or competing in an official meet.

LEARNING EXPERIENCE—UNDERSTANDING THE RULES

1. Observe a fencing competition to note the application of various fencing rules. Question competent directors on the nuances of rule interpretations.

2. Refer to other strategies that deal with rules, thereby expanding your understanding and application of the rules.
3. Check past issues of the guide books of the National Association for Girls and Women in Sports. Take the tests included in several such guides to see how well you know and understand the rules.
4. Refer to the rules manual of the Amateur Fencers League of America for further refinements of the rules.

HIGHLIGHTS

1. Describe a fencing strip, giving its dimensions and stating the purposes of the lines on the strip.
2. State the penalties imposed for crossing both the lateral and end boundaries of a strip.
3. List the officials and state each one's main responsibility.
4. Describe the orderly sequence for starting a bout.
5. Explain how the winner is determined.
6. Explain how a tie is resolved.
7. Explain the rule of right of way.

5

Developing Additional Skills

Concept: Additional Attacks, Parries, Ripostes, Preparatory Actions, Time Actions, and Footwork Will Add Interest, Variety, Excitement, and Competitive Skill to a Fencer's Game.

Many years ago fencing masters would insist that beginners spend at least a year on fundamental movements. Only after an adequate period of practice and instruction would a novice be allowed to compete in a tournament. This policy was intended to allow sufficient time for molding the "correct" habits to "assure" top performance. But no two individuals respond alike. Therefore, the perception of what are *correct habits* and what are not *exactly correct* is subjective and tends to be determined either by the pleasing aesthetic qualities of a fencer's movements, by the fencer's success, or by both. The aesthetic quality or "proper" form may take years of practice for some to acquire, and only a short time for others.

Only when the fundamentals have been well learned should a fencer move on to new skills; and no matter how skilled or successful a fencer becomes, it is necessary to review and hone the fundamental movements frequently. Programs of advanced skills aim to improve actions already learned, to increase the repertoire of actions, and to develop confidence and the ability for self-analysis.

New skills and techniques, whether on a beginning or advanced level, should be related to the total game as quickly as possible by adopting these general principles:

(a) Observe the component parts of the skill and observe similarities to skills already learned.
(b) Know how, when, and why the skill is used.
   1. Observe yourself in a mirror while performing the skills.
   2. Add footwork (advance, retreat, lunge) to each new hand skill so that foot and hand movements are coordinated.
   3. Increase the tempo of the movements.
   4. Know all possible responses the opponent might make and practice counter responses.
   5. Practice the newly acquired skill when bouting in class. A skill used many times becomes part of the fencer.
(c) Execute the skill, aspiring to technical perfection and tactical correctness.

Low-line attacks are directed at the target area below the bell guard.

With the advent of electrical fencing, low-line attacks and parries have become popular, necessary, and effective. Even though a foil point directed under the arm may not be visible to the fencer, the hit will be detected by the electrical scoring machine which signals the president that a hit has been made. For this reason many instructors feel the low-line attacks and parries should be taught early in the fencing progression. The authors of this book feel that low-line attacks and parries should not be included in a beginning course. Generally a few skills well learned will enable the beginning fencer to progress more rapidly.

The low line is the area beneath the bell guard. The outside low line (directly below 6 position) is 8 (octave); the inside low line (directly below 4 position) is 7 (septime).

ATTACK IN LOW LINE

Attacks to the low line are generally made as follows:

(a) When the opponent's foil hand is high.
(b) When a change in strategy is indicated.
(c) When a fencer wants to open the high line by drawing the opponent into the low line.

To execute low-line attacks, direct the point below the opponent's guard toward the elbow. The arm is lowered with the final movement. The blade should bend *laterally* on contact with the target to avoid the opponent's arm. The blade will bend laterally if the fencer finishes with the hand in supination (for an attack to 7) or pronation (for an attack to 8).

LEARNING EXPERIENCE—LOW-LINE ATTACKS

1. *Engage blades in 6.*
   Fencer A—Disengage into low line, lunge, and score. (Execute with footwork.)
2. *Engage blades in 4.*
   Fencer A—Disengage into low line, lunge, and score. (Execute with footwork.)

In a semicircular parry, the point of the weapon describes a sweeping arc (a nearly semicircular movement) as the blade moves from the high line to the low line or vice versa. There are two low-line parries—7 (septime) and 8 (octave).

Parry 8 (octave): When engaged in 6 and threatened by a low-line attack, the fencer should parry by describing a near semicircle or arc with the point moving counterclockwise. The hand is supinated throughout the parry. Riposte either to the low line or the high line.

Parry 7 (septime): When engaged in 4 and threatened in the low line, the fencer should parry by describing a near semicircle or arc with the point moving clockwise. In 7 the arc is rounder because it sweeps the point off target. The hand is supinated throughout the parry. Riposte either the low line or the high line.

PARRY 7   PARRY 8

The various combinations of semicircular parries are from 6 to 8, from 8 to 6, from 4 to 7, and from 7 to 4. Combinations of 6 to 7 and 4 to 8 are not suggested since a diagonal movement may cause a fencer to miss contacting the attacking blade.

LEARNING EXPERIENCE—LOW-LINE PARRIES

1. Engage blades in 6.
   Fencer A—Disengage into 4.
   Fencer B—Semicircular parry 8 (and riposte).
2. Engage blades in 8.
   Fencer A—Disengage into high line.
   Fencer B—Parry 6 by executing semicircular movement (and riposte).

A compound attack consists of one or more feints combined with a simple attack and may be used when a simple attack fails to score.

A fencer must gain distance on his opponent at the beginning of the attack with the initiation of the feint. To resemble the real attack the feint must penetrate as deeply as possible, threatening the target before the fencer starts the final action.

Having learned in Chapter 3 the direct thrust, the disengage, and the cutover, a fencer has established the foundation for the compound attacks. Developing and successfully executing them will require practice to coordinate the blade movements, the weapon-arm extension, and the footwork. As a fencer becomes more adept in using compound attacks, the partner should concentrate on increasing the speed of the parry, making an honest effort to contact the fencer's blade.

Illustrations of compound attacks are discussed below:

The one-two attack consists of two disengages. The first disengage is a feint into the open line. The second disengage deceives the opponent's lateral parry; that is, as the opponent parries the disengage, the fencer evades the parry by returning to or disengaging into the original line of engagement.

The shortest distance between two points is a straight line. Apply this axiom to the one-two. The blade and arm move straight forward. Use only the fingers to lower and raise the point. When the one-two has been learned, it can be combined with other basic skills.

LEARNING EXPERIENCE—ONE-TWO ATTACK

1. Engage blades in 6.
   Fencer A—Disengage feint into 4.
   Fencer B—Parry 4.
   Fencer A—Disengage into 6, evading the parry, and score.
2. Engage blades in 4.
   Fencer A—Disengage feint into 6.
   Fencer B—Parry 6.
   Fencer A—Disengage into 4, evading the parry, and score.

Low-high and high-low attacks. These are designed to deceive the semicircular parries. The low-high attack is begun from an engagement in the high line. The feint to the low line is directed beneath and parallel to the opponent's arm. As the opponent executes the semicircular parry, the fencer should deceive the blade by disengaging into the high line. The high-low attack starts from an engagement in the low line. The feint is made to the high line. The fencer should deceive the opponent's parry, scoring in the low line.

Doublé. Used to deceive a circular parry, the doublé is a two-part attack. The first action is a disengage feint intended to draw the opponent's circular parry. The second action is a circular motion to deceive the circular parry. The blade should remain ahead of the opponent's circular movement while progressing toward the target. The fencer's point describes a continuous circle and a half, ending in the same line into which the feint was made.

LEARNING EXPERIENCE—DOUBLÉ ATTACK

1. *Engage blades in 6.*
   Fencer A—Disengage feint into 4.
   Fencer B—Circular 6 parry.
   Fencer A—Deceive the parry, and score.
2. *Engage blades in 4.*
   Fencer A—Disengage feint into 6.
   Fencer B—Circular 4 parry.
   Fencer A—Deceive the parry, and score.

Direct thrust, cutover (coupé). This is an attack intended to draw the opponent's parry with a feint (direct thrust), to deceive the parry, and to attack the opened line with a cutover. Since it requires more time to perform than does the disengage, execute the final movement sharply and quickly over the tip of the opponent's blade.

LEARNING EXPERIENCE—FEINT THRUST, CUTOVER ATTACK

1. *Fencers practice with absence of blades (no blade contact).*
   Fencer A—Feint with direct thrust.
   Fencer B—Parry 4 or 6.
   Fencer A—Cutover into 6 or 4, deceiving the parry, and score.
2. *Fencers practice with absence of blades (no blade contact).*
   Fencer A—Feint with direct thrust.
   Fencer B—Parry circular 4 or circular 6.
   Fencer A—Cutover into 4 or 6, deceiving the parry, and score.

A compound riposte consists of one or more feints while making the riposte.

To successfully execute the compound riposte, a fencer should delay the lunge, allowing sufficient time in which to complete the feint(s). The compound riposte has many variations built around the *extension,* the *disengage,* and the *cutover.* The primary difference between compound attacks and compound ripostes is that in the former the weapon arm is more fully extended in the feints, while in the latter the weapon arm is extended only on the final movement. (A compound fencing action, whether an attack or a riposte, is merely a combination of simple actions.)

LEARNING EXPERIENCE—COMPOUND RIPOSTE

1. Engage blades in 6.
   Fencer A—Attack with a disengage.
   Fencer B—Parry with circular 6.
   Fencer A—Anticipating direct riposte, parry 6.
   Fencer B—Deceive parry 6, feint with a disengage (one).
   Fencer A—Parry 4.
   Fencer B—Deceive parry 4 with a disengage (two), extend the arm, and score.
2. Engage blades in 6.
   Fencer A—Attack with a disengage.
   Fencer B—Parry with circular 6.
   Fencer A—Anticipating direct riposte, parry 6.
   Fencer B—Deceive parry 6, feint with a disengage.
   Fencer A—Parry circular 6.
   Fencer B—Deceive circular 6 by doubling through with final movement, extend the arm, and score.

The reprise, remise, and the redoublement are renewed attacks which are executed against an opponent whose parry and/or riposte is not decisive.

A fencer who doggedly pursues and renews an attack will score many more touches than the fencer who attacks and, missing or falling short, breaks off the attack and recovers before initiating another attack.

Reprise is a retaking or renewal of the attack, and is used against an opponent who fails or hesitates to riposte. After lunging, recover either forward or backward, depending upon whether or not the opponent retreats, and lunge again.

LEARNING EXPERIENCE—REPRISE

Engage blades in 6.
Fencer A—Disengage and lunge.
Fencer B—Retreat.
Fencer A—Recover forward to on-guard position, lunge, and score.

Remise is a replacement of the point on the target made while the attacker is still in the lunge. It is used against an opponent who parries but hesitates, who fails to riposte, or who uses compound ripostes. Immediately following the opponent's parry, the point is directed into the same line as the original attack without additional blade or arm movement.

LEARNING EXPERIENCE—REMISE

Engage blades in 6.
Fencer A—Disengage and lunge.
Fencer B—Parry 4 and return to central guard position without riposting.
Fencer A—Replace point on target in the 4 line.

Redoublement is a new *indirect* attack (either disengage or cutover), executed while a fencer is still in the lunge, against an opponent who delays or fails to riposte.

LEARNING EXPERIENCE—REDOUBLEMENT

Engage blades in 6.
Fencer A—Disengage and lunge.
Fencer B—Parry 4 and hold the parry.
Fencer A—While in lunge, disengage and score.

The taking of the blade defines a movement which deflects the opponent's blade while maintaining contact with it.

One such movement has been covered in Chapter 3—the engagement, which is the contact made by crossing blades.

The *bind* is a controlling action executed against an extended blade. Leverage must be exerted by contacting the middle or weak part of the opponent's blade with the strong part of the fencer's own blade. The opponent's blade is then carried diagonally across the body from high line to low line or vice versa. As the point is moved over the opponent's extended blade, the fencer's blade is extended while executing the bind.

The principle of the bind is as follows: the blades are engaged. If a fencer begins the bind from 4, the blade should finish covering the 8 position; if a fencer begins from 8, the blade should finish covering the 4 position. If a fencer begins from 6, the blade should finish covering the 7 position; if begun from 7, the blade should finish covering the 6 position.

LEARNING EXPERIENCE—THE BIND

Engage blades in 6.
Fencer A—Extend the blade.
Fencer B—Bind over the blade and carry it to 7.

The *croisé* is a half bind which carries the blade vertically from the high line to the low line (not from the low line to the high line—a movement easily deceived). The fencer, starting from an engagement of 4, presses down on the opponent's blade by lowering the wrist and forearm. Maintaining contact with the blade and keeping the hand supinated, the fencer should hit the opponent's flank. With the blades engaged, the principle of the croisé is as follows: If a fencer begins the croisé from 4, the blade will finish covering the 7 position. If a fencer begins from 6, the blade will finish covering the 8 position. Use the same drills for both the bind and the croisé.

The *envelopment* is a double bind in which the blade is returned to the original line of engagement, with the fencer maintaining control over the opponent's blade throughout the execution. The movement is most easily executed when fencers are engaged in 6. The envelopment is accomplished by executing two binds in quick succession.

LEARNING EXPERIENCE—THE ENVELOPMENT

Engage blades in 6.
Fencer A—Extend the blade.
Fencer B—Envelop the blade and score, holding the opponent's foible (weak blade section) with one's own forte (strong blade section), completing the movement and scoring with a glide, straight thrust.

The attack with second intention is a false attack to lure the opponent into parrying and riposting.

The fencer parries the opponent's riposte and scores with a counterattack. Convincing the opponent that the initial action is the real attack requires the fencer to develop a sense of timing and distance, strong defense, and a quick offense.

LEARNING EXPERIENCE—SECOND INTENTION

Engage blades in 6.
Fencer A—Disengage lunge as false attack.
Fencer B—Parry 4 and riposte.
Fencer A—Parry 4, riposte, and score.

The time action is a counteroffensive movement which may steal the fencing tempo from the opponent's attack and give the right of way to the other fencer.

Examples of time action are the *stop hit* and the *stop hit with opposition*. The *stop hit* is executed by extending the blade toward the target as the opponent initiates a compound attack. To steal the time and gain the right of way, the *stop hit* must arrive before the attacker has begun the final movement of the attack. If the *stop hit*

THE FLECHE ATTACK

1

2

3

is used against a simple attack, and if both the *stop hit* and the simple attack arrive simultaneously, the counterattacker will be declared hit. A *stop hit with opposition* is executed by closing the line and extending into the opponent's attack. Proper execution of the *stop hit* and the *stop hit with opposition* requires the fencer to seize the correct moment to launch the counterattack, then to follow through without hesitation and without telegraphing the intent. When there is doubt as to whether the original attack or the *stop hit* has the right of way, the decision will generally be in favor of the original attack.

Advanced footwork enables a fencer to execute a balestra lunge and a flèche attack.

The *balestra* (jump) is similar to the advance but is performed more explosively and quickly. The fencer starts the balestra by forcefully swinging (extending) the leading foreleg without elevating the leading knee. As the leading leg descends, the rear foot is quickly moved forward a distance equal to that covered by the leading foot. Both feet should land simultaneously.

LEARNING EXPERIENCE—THE BALESTRA

1. *Observe yourself in a mirror. As you perform the balestra, do you move toward your opponent in a plane parallel to the floor or do you jump in a parabolic manner? How much of the sole of your leading foot can you see in the mirror? The higher you elevate your foot, the slower you execute the balestra, giving your opponent the opportunity to employ a time action against you.*
2. *Extend your weapon arm as you practice the balestra, followed immediately by a lunge. Check your performance in the mirror.*

The *flèche* is a running attack which should be used very cautiously. Failure to score in this all-out effort leaves a fencer vulnerable to the opponent's counterattack. According to the rules, a fencer may not score after passing the opponent— that is, after reversing one's fencing position; the opponent, however, has one opportunity to score by executing an immediate counterattack.

The projected angle of the body must closely correspond to the direction of thrust from both legs before the fencer takes off from the floor and before the rear leg crosses the leading leg. To avoid forewarning the start of the attack, use slight body feints by shifting the weight imperceptibly forward and backward in no set pattern. The rear leg initiates the flèche, but the ball of the leading foot provides the explosive impulse that is needed to drive the fencer toward the opponent and off the floor. The extension of the leading leg immediately follows the driving action. As in running, the rear leg then crosses over the leading leg, helping the fencer regain balance and pass rather than collide with the opponent.

A fencer should avoid body contact with the opponent. The rules clearly define and forbid jostling one's adversary. Infraction of the rule may result in a warning, loss of a touch and/or score, and/or expulsion from the competition.

LEARNING EXPERIENCE—THE FLECHE ATTACK

1. Practice in slow motion the following sequence of movements, starting from the on-guard position:
   a. Shift weight to the leading foot and extend weapon arm.
   b. Extend the rear leg.
   c. Push off from the ball of the leading foot.
   d. Extend the leading leg and propel the body obliquely forward.
   e. Cross the rear leg over the leading leg.
   f. Run past your opponent.
2. Repeat above movements with increasing speed.

Speed and simplicity are paramount in fencing today. Avoid becoming enamored with highly involved movements except as an exercise for developing quick responses and facile fingerplay.

After acquiring skills and knowledge, fence often and against many opponents—both right-handed and left-handed. It is through bouting that fencers can develop their skills and test their analytical ability, timing, sense of distance, and speed.

HIGHLIGHTS

1. Explain how to relate and adapt new skills and techniques to your game.
2. Demonstrate a low-line attack to 8 and to 7 on another fencer.
3. Name and demonstrate the two semicircular or low-line parries.
4. Demonstrate that you know how to execute each compound attack.
5. Define a compound riposte and demonstrate one type.
6. Explain and demonstrate what is meant by a renewed attack and give three examples of such attacks.
7. Explain what is meant by "the taking of the blade."
8. Compare and contrast verbally and by demonstration the bind, the croisé, and the envelopment.
9. Describe and show the attack with second intention.
10. With an opponent, demonstrate the proper timing and tempo for executing time actions.
11. Explain and demonstrate the difference between a balestra and an advance.
12. Explain what precautions a fencer must take in executing a flèche attack.

6

Strategy

Concept: The Basic Strategy in Fencing Is to Hit the Opponent and Avoid Being Hit.

A fencer should have a plan of action before approaching the fencing strip. Upon completion of the bout, it is good practice to review and analyze the action.

To develop strategy for bouting, a fencer should master certain prerequisites.

The first step is to learn the fundamental skills. A beginner usually is eager to cross blades and bout. Many instructors permit this early in the learning stage to illustrate that learning fundamental skills is essential to success. Most instructors

51

insist that experienced fencers, as well as beginners, include a review of fundamentals in their daily programs.

Continual improvement leading to mastery of basic skills is an integral part of any fencing program. When the fencer's execution of fundamentals becomes conditioned reflexes, complete attention can then be centered on the plan of action, or strategy. Controlled movements can be made only if the movements have been mastered; lack of control leads to irrational actions.

Fencing requires stamina. Useless expenditure of energy can lead to early fatigue. Executing movements correctly will conserve energy by avoiding wasted motion.

Mastering fundamentals provides a base on which to build a repertoire of movements. All compound fencing phrases are merely a series of simple moves made in proper sequence, time, and distance. Unless simple movements are first mastered, a fencer cannot hope to execute complex actions successfully.

The second step is to learn, understand, and apply the rules of fencing. Rules are designed to create a safe, suitable, and equitable bouting environment. Ignorance of rules results in uncertainty and insecurity. For example, Fencer A has initiated an attack that strikes the opponent on a valid target. Fencer B also scores. The director (the president) declares a touch against Fencer A. If the rule of right of way is misunderstood, the fencer may not comprehend the decision. What Fencer A may have thought was an effective attack was not deemed so by the director. Fencer A may now hesitate using that attack again—or any attack for that matter. (See Chapter 4 on the rule of right of way, pp. 37–38.)

Ignorance is, of course, no excuse for violating fencing rules. When entering a competition, a fencer is bound by the rules and regulations governing that competition. The official amateur rules for divisional, sectional, and national competitions (in the United States) are based on the international rules and are periodically published by the Amateur Fencers League of America. College and university conferences operate under slightly modified AFLA rules. These modifications usually relate to the time limits, ground rules, and structure of competitions. The rules governing the validity of hits are the same worldwide.

The third step is to develop endurance and stamina. In a competition of short duration, endurance may be less important than skill and technique; however, its importance becomes obvious in extended competition.

The body will perform more efficiently if given proper care. Both physical conditioning and skills training are imperative in developing fencing ability. The former involves exercise, proper diet, adequate sleep, and abstinence from drugs, smoking, and intoxicating beverages. The latter refers to the development of fencing skills through regular instruction and practice.

LEARNING EXPERIENCE—BODY CONDITIONING

1. *How much warm-up do you require before competition begins? Between bouts? Some fencers require more than others. Determine your own needs.*
2. *How do diet and sleep affect your endurance and stamina? You must determine*

your own requirements and methods of maintaining top condition.
3. Discuss dietary requirements with a qualified nutritionist.

The fourth step is to observe the protocol of the game.   By observing protocol, a
fencer will earn the respect of opponents, officials, and spectators.

A fencer answering "Yes" to the following questions has learned fencing protocol.

1. Do you dress properly in clean fencing clothes?
2. Do you have an extra weapon handy in case of a breakdown so time will not be
   wasted?
3. Do you offer your assistance in hooking up the electrical equipment? In scoring?
   In timing? In judging?
4. Are you ready to fence when your bout is called?
5. Do you salute your opponent before the bout begins and shake hands at the
   conclusion of the bout?
6. Do you avoid alibiing or rationalizing?
7. Do you know how to request time out?
8. Do you thank the director and judges at the conclusion of a match?

To further enhance fencing strategy, tactical competence must be developed.

*The first step in acquiring tactical competence is to understand and assess one's
abilities.*   Some fencers never learn to rely upon their own judgment. They need to
be told what to do and when to do it. A fencer should learn to think analytically by
doing the following:

1. *Recognize your strengths and weaknesses and try to capitalize on them.* Use
those defensive maneuvers that have proven to be most successful. An aggressive
competitor should emphasize attacks. However, be ready to parry and counterattack. An extremely cautious fencer should strengthen defense by using ripostes and
counter-time actions.

2. *Understand the possible responses to an action.* Each opponent will react to a
threat in one of three ways: by retreating, by attacking, or by holding ground. If the
opponent retreats, the response may be to pursue and score. If the opponent
attacks, the response may be either to stop hit with opposition or to parry and
riposte. If the opponent is holding ground, the response may be to attack to score.
If the attack is not successful, be prepared to execute a secondary action.

3. *Employ diverse tactics that force the opponent to readjust and reassess
strategy.* It is advisable to probe the opponent with feints directed at all lines in
order to seek out normal responses. If a particular attack is scoring, continue to use
it. As soon as it fails to score, attempt a different attack, but return to the original
attack later in the bout.

4. *Develop self-confidence.* A fencer must be willing to take some risks in order
to score, but once the decision to take a calculated risk is made, one should be
totally committed to that action, believing it will succeed. An opponent frequently
feels as much threatened by a fencer's confidence as by the weapon point.

5. *Control the distance.* To avoid being hit by an opponent's attack, a fencer may employ three methods: deflect the blade from the target; remove the target by retreating; or use a combination of both.

Some fencers require a great distance in which to coordinate a smooth, composed attack. They depend, too, on the opponent retreating. Occasionally, to abort an attack, a fencer should hold ground as the opponent advances. This not only decreases the distance required, but also interrupts the tempo.

When a fencer has reached the warning line, 1 meter from the end of the mat, the president halts the bout and warns the fencer. The bout is then resumed. If, after having been warned, the fencer goes off the end of the mat with both feet, a touch will be registered.

Few fencers feel comfortable when they are in warning. Yet this position can be used to advantage if overeagerness causes the opponent to miscalculate the distance.

Good balance and position are a part of distance control. It is of no benefit to be at the right distance or to use the correct move at the appropriate time if lack of balance prevents scoring.

6. *Develop a feeling for tempo.* Every fencing movement has a rhythm (cadence) that can be used to advantage by either fencer. For example, many fencers try to mesmerize the opponent by making slow, hypnotic movements with the foil to establish a rhythm. At the right moment the fencer strikes with decisiveness and rapidity, and the opponent is scored upon before being able to react. To avoid becoming the victim of such mesmerism, vary the pace of the movements so the opponent is unable to find a pattern to the tempo. Reversing the above example may sometimes be effective. By making quick, staccato movements, the opponent will be led to expect a lightning-fast attack. Find an opening and score by making a slower, more deliberate attack.

The next step in acquiring tactical competence is to understand and assess the opponent. A fencer must realize an opponent changes strategy from time to time. Watch the opponent bout with others and observe any habits or patterns. It is easier to take advantage of these than to force a change.

A fencer should determine the following regarding an opponent:

1. What is the opponent's measure?
2. Are the opponent's parries controlled and well conceived? Can the blade be deceived?
3. How much distance does the opponent cover when lunging? How quickly is the lunge and recovery executed?
4. Are the opponent's attack movements telegraphed? For example: Do the fingers of the trailing hand wiggle? Does the shoulder droop? Or is the on-guard position deepened just prior to attacking?

Each situation calls for a slightly different response. The greater a fencer's experience and knowledge, the more intelligent will be the response. Regard the opponent as a puzzle to be solved in the fewest possible movements.

The attacker usually has greater opportunity to score than the defender. Thus, attacking strategy becomes clear—*press the opponent with attacks. Attack with vigor and decisive commitment.* Hesitation may lose the right of way. It is advisable to be unpredictable, varying the attacks so there will be no discernible pattern.

The third step in acquiring tactical competence is to understand and assess the jury.   Many a disgruntled fencer has walked off a strip defeated, failing to understand the rulings.

Learn to listen to the director's interpretations of fencing actions and use this information to plan tactics. To avoid doubtful touches or simultaneous actions, score in such a way that there can be no possible question as to who has the right of way. Avoid questioning a decision that involves the judgment of the director.

When conventional weapons are used and judges determine the materiality of a hit, it is best if a fencer in no way indicates agreement or disagreement with the judges' voting. Avoid showing anger or disgust on the strip. The jury and the spectators may take this as a sign of disrespect. A wise fencer will not discuss a decision with the opponent during or immediately after a bout.

The fourth step in acquiring tactical competence is to understand and assess the environment.   The physical environment is generally beyond a fencer's control. However, awareness of the physical factors that might affect performance will prepare the fencer to cope with them. A fencer should determine the following regarding environmental factors:

1. Is the lighting better on one end of the strip than on the other?
2. Are the strips too close to one another? Is sufficient end space allowed? Are there any physical obstructions?
3. Are conditions satisfactory for executing a flèche (running attack)?
4. Of what material is the fencing surface made? Does it provide suitable traction?
5. Is the audience apt to be partisan and vocal?
6. Is the room temperature comfortable for competitors?
7. If electrical apparatus is being used, have the reels, body cords, and other equipment been checked?

LEARNING EXPERIENCE—SUGGESTED RESPONSES TO FENCING SITUATIONS

1. *Each opponent will exhibit some habitual characteristics. The list below is in no way exhaustive, but it provides suggested responses to some specific situations.*
   a. *The bout has just started.*
      1. *Learn the habitual parries of the opponent by using false attacks to expose reactions.*
      2. *Learn the speed of the opponent in the same manner.*
      3. *Learn the distance of the opponent by inviting attacks.*
   b. *The opponent has a low guard.*
      1. *Attack to high line.*
      2. *Feint high, hit low on reaction.*
      3. *Beat blade, attack high.*
   c. *The opponent maintains an extended arm.*
      1. *Beat.*
      2. *Pressure.*

        3. Glide.

        4. Bind.

        5. Envelop.

  d. The opponent habitually stop thrusts.

        1. Perform simple attacks.

        2. Attack with opposition.

        3. False attack, parry the stop hit, riposte.

  e. The opponent offers invitations.

        1. Extend and advance with caution until opponent returns to on-guard.

        2. Feint, then deceive opponent's attempt to contact the blade.

        3. Use simple attack only if in distance.

  f. The opponent uses Italian style (straps weapon to wrist, dominates blade).

        1. Fence with absence of blades.

        2. Permit opponent to attack—use strong circular parries.

  g. The opponent does not respond to feints.

        1. Perform simple attack with all-out effort.

        2. Seek reactions to actions on the blade.

        3. Invite attack, and parry riposte.

  h. The opponent is of short stature.

        1. Stay out of opponent's reach.

        2. Use stop hits.

  i. The opponent is of tall stature.

        1. Gain distance cautiously.

        2. Use aggressive actions on the blade.

        3. Use attacks of second intention.

        4. Get inside the point to fence at close quarters.

  j. The opponent has a weak defense.

        1. Use varied attacks.

        2. False attack, remise, or replacement.

        3. Use reprise.

  k. The opponent is left-handed.

        1. Draw the opponent into the 4 guard position and deceive the circular 4 parries.

        2. End attacks in opponent's 6 line.

        3. Feint low outside, hit high.

        4. Attack with a change beat-cutover.

2. Observe an intercollegiate, national, or club competition. What offensive techniques were employed? What style of defense was used? Were counter actions used? How were these various actions executed?

3. Observe the techniques employed by the director (president). Did the director know the rules? Were the calls consistent? Was the bout kept under control? How would you evaluate the director's performance?

4. Keep a notebook in which you describe and analyze the styles and actions of your opponents.

5. At the conclusion of each bout, record how each fencer scored and determine appropriate counter movements. Also, record the strategy employed to score.

HIGHLIGHTS

1. Explain the basic strategy of fencing.
2. Explain how basic skills, rules, and protocol are related to strategy.
3. List the advantages to be gained by thoroughly learning the fundamental skills.
4. Explain the effect of endurance and stamina.
5. What organization publishes the rules of amateur fencing?
6. List five rules of protocol a fencer should observe.
7. Describe how you would respond to an opponent who retreats, attacks, or holds ground.
8. Describe three maneuvers to avoid a hit.
9. Explain how fencing distance can be used to advantage.
10. In developing strategy, what steps can be taken to assess yourself, the opponent, the jury, and the environment?

7

The Role of Officials
in Competition

Concept: Officiating Is a Skill Acquired through Study, Observation, and Experience.

Despite the need for developing competent officials, officiating is a most neglected aspect of fencing. Classes, clinics, and workshops can help develop a better understanding of the basic rules and increase skill in the techniques and mechanics of officiating. Learning to officiate should be a part of every beginner's training because it helps fencers understand how decisions are made and because fencers are often called upon to officiate.

A fencer should develop the skills and personal characteristics necessary for officiating.

These include the following:

(a) Knowledge, interpretation, and application of the rules.
(b) Prompt reaction: registering decisions quickly.
(c) Self-confidence.

(d) Consistency in judgment: realizing the significance of every action, being unbiased, and registering the same decisions for instances exactly alike.
(e) Creditable behavior: developing self-control in order to establish and maintain rapport with fencers, coaches, officials, and spectators.
(f) Well-groomed physical appearance.
(g) Good physical condition in order to move with the action.

The successful application of these characteristics is often affected by the director's *style* in controlling the bout with as little interference as possible.

When using conventional (nonelectrical) equipment, the officiating jury includes a president (director) and four judges. Other officials are a scorekeeper and a timekeeper.

The president has complete control over the fencers, coaches, officials, and spectators.   The president's duties are to award hits according to the rules, to see that order is maintained, to observe the actions of both fencers, and to clearly interpret these actions to the judges.

The judges are responsible for determining whether or not a hit has been made.   Two of the judges (1 and 2 in the illustration) are on the president's right to observe hits against the fencer on the president's left. Judges 3 and 4 observe hits on the opposing fencer.

The jury assumes positions around the strip and the fencers without interfering with the action. To insure safety the judges stand about 3 feet (1 meter) from the edge of the strip and 3 feet behind the nearest competitor. They move with the competitors to insure an unobstructed view of the action and assigned target.

As soon as a judge observes a valid or invalid (off-target) hit on the fencer whom he is watching, the judge must *immediately* raise an arm overhead to advise the president, who will halt the bout. If necessary, the president briefly reconstructs the actions that composed the last fencing phrase prior to the call of "Halt," analyzes

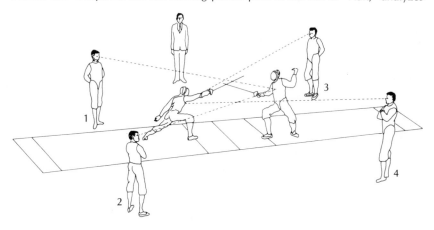

POSITIONING OF JURY MEMBERS

them, and questions the judges for their opinions. When questioned, the judges must reply promptly and decisively by voting one of the following: (1) "Yes." (2) "Off target." (3) "No." (4) "I abstain."

The president votes last. The opinion of each judge counts as one vote, while the president's opinion has a value of one and a half votes. By abstaining, an official indicates uncertainty, consequently no point value.

LEARNING EXPERIENCE

Fencer A attacks Fencer B. Judges 1 and 2, watching Fencer B, raise their arms. The president halts the bout. Reviewing the action, the president asks: "The attack?" Judges 1 and 2 vote "Yes." What is the decision? (Fencer B is hit.)

If the judges on the same end (1 and 2 or 3 and 4) agree (either by saying "Yes," "No," or "Off target"), their judgment prevails.

LEARNING EXPERIENCE

Fencer A attacks Fencer B. Judge 1 raises an arm. The president halts the bout. Reviewing the action, the president asks: "The attack?" Judge 1 votes "Yes." Judge 2 votes "I abstain." President votes "No." What is the decision? (No score.)

If one of the judges has a definite opinion and the other abstains, the opinion of the president, whose vote is overriding, prevails. If the president also abstains, the decision of the judge with a definite opinion prevails.

LEARNING EXPERIENCE

Fencer A attacks Fencer B. Judge 1 raises an arm. The president halts the bout. Reviewing the action, the president asks: "The attack?" Judge 1 votes "Yes." Judge 2 votes "No." The president votes "I abstain." What is the decision? (Doubtful hit or benefit of doubt—no score.)

If the two judges at the same end (1 and 2 or 3 and 4) are positive but have contrary opinions or if both abstain, the president casts the determining vote. If the president also abstains, the hit is regarded as doubtful, and there is no score. A doubtful hit is never scored against a competitor. Also, any hit must be annulled if made subsequently or simultaneously in the same phrase by the fencer receiving the benefit of the doubt. However, in the case of a hit made by the fencer who made the doubtful hit, the following will apply: *A subsequent hit must be scored if made by the fencer who made the doubtful hit without any hit having been made by the opponent.*

LEARNING EXPERIENCE

Fencer A attacks Fencer B, who parries and ripostes. Fencer A parries the riposte and counterattacks. Judges 1 and 2 raise their arms. The president halts the bout. Reviewing the action, the president asks: "The original attack by Fencer A?" Judge 1 votes "Yes." Judge 2 votes "No." The President votes "I abstain." The president asks: "The riposte?" Judges 3 and 4 vote "No." The president votes "I abstain." The president then asks: "The counterattack by Fencer A?" Judges 1 and 2 vote "Yes." What is the decision? (Fencer B is hit.)

If there is doubt concerning the validity of the hit but not that there was a hit (that is, one "Yes" and one "Off target"), no other hit in this phrase can be scored.

LEARNING EXPERIENCE

Fencer A attacks Fencer B, who ripostes. Judges 1, 2, 3, and 4 raise their arms. The president halts the bout. Reviewing the action, the president asks: "The original attack by Fencer A?" Judge 1 votes "Yes." Judge 2 votes "Off target." The president votes "I abstain." The President then asks: "The riposte?" Judges 3 and 4 vote "Yes." What is the decision? (No score.)

The timekeeper notifies the president when one minute of fencing time remains and terminates the bout at the end of that minute. The president halts the bout, notifies the fencers of the one-minute warning, and states the score. At the end of that minute, the timekeeper, and no other official, terminates the bout verbally or by use of a horn, whistle, or bell.

The scorekeeper is responsible for maintaining an accurate record of the scoring. Individual tournament bouts are usually conducted by means of round-robin competition within pools composed of four or more competitors. Frequently the number of entries requires several pools. In this case, the fencers scoring highest in each pool advance to the next round, where new pools are formed. This round-robin process continues until a final pool is attained. Round-robin bouting in this final pool determines the winner. The number of qualifiers from one round to the next (those who advance from one pool to the next) is determined prior to the start of competition, and the order of bouting is governed by a fixed schedule prepared in advance.

Each fencer is represented by a number corresponding to those in the vertical and horizontal columns on the scoresheet. The order of bouts depends on the number of fencers in the pool (see the illustration, Order of Bouts). For example, in a pool of four competitors the first bout would be between Fencer A (number 1) and Fencer D (number 4). The scorekeeper divides the scoreboxes horizontally in half and uses the lower part to record hits scored and the upper part to record victory (V) or defeat (D). Total victories are recorded in the V (victory) column.

The standing or place of each fencer at the completion of a pool is determined by the number of victories. If two or more fencers who might normally qualify for the next round have an equal number of victories, their standing is determined by a barrage (fence-off) or by an indicator using the following formula: hits scored minus

OFFICIAL SCORE SHEET

WEAPON_____

COMPETITION_____

POOL_____STRIP_____

DATE_____

DIRECTOR_____

BARRAGE	NO.	1	2	3	4	V	HG/HR	IND	PL
	1	■							
	2		■						
	3			■					
	4				■				

CLUB	FENCER	NO.	1	2	3	4	5	6	7	8	9	10	V	HG/HR	IND	PL
		1	■													
		2		■												
		3			■											
		4				■										
		5					■									
		6						■								
		7							■							
		8								■						
		9									■					
		10										■				
		HG														

ORDER OF BOUTS

4 FENCERS — 6 BOUTS

1—4	
2—3	
1—3	
2—4	
3—4	
1—2	

5 FENCERS — 10 BOUTS

1—2
3—4
5—1
2—3
5—4
1—3
2—5
4—1
3—5
4—2

6 FENCERS — 15 BOUTS

1—4	6—4
2—5	1—2
3—6	3—4
5—1	5—6
4—2	2—3
3—1	1—6
6—2	4—5
5—3	

7 FENCERS — 21 BOUTS

1—4	3—1
2—5	4—6
3—6	7—2
7—1	3—5
5—4	1—6
2—3	2—4
6—7	7—3
5—1	6—5
4—3	1—2
6—2	4—7
5—7	

8 FENCERS — 28 BOUTS

2—3	8—3	3—7
1—5	6—7	4—8
7—4	4—2	2—6
6—8	8—1	3—5
1—2	7—5	1—7
3—4	3—6	4—6
5—6	2—8	8—5
8—7	5—4	7—2
4—1	6—1	1—3
5—2		

9 FENCERS — 36 BOUTS

1—9	1—2	3—1	4—1
2—8	9—3	2—4	5—3
3—7	8—4	5—9	6—2
4—6	7—5	8—6	9—7
1—5	6—1	7—1	1—8
2—9	3—2	4—3	4—5
8—3	9—4	5—2	3—6
7—4	5—8	6—9	2—7
6—5	7—6	8—7	9—8

10 FENCERS — 45 BOUTS

1—4	7—8	3—4	8—1	6—4
6—9	5—1	8—9	7—4	9—5
2—5	10—6	5—10	9—3	10—3
7—10	4—2	1—6	2—6	7—1
3—1	9—7	2—7	5—8	4—8
8—6	5—3	3—8	4—10	2—9
4—5	10—8	4—9	1—9	3—6
9—10	1—2	6—5	3—7	5—7
2—3	6—7	10—2	8—2	1—10

MULTIPLE TEAM MATES IN A POOL

POOL OF 6		POOL OF 8	
3 Team Mates *1-2-3	4 Team Mates *1-2-4-5	3 Team Mates *1-2-3	4 Team Mates *1-2-3-5
1—2 5—3	1—4 4—2	2—3 3—7	2—3 6—1
4—5 1—6	2—5 1—6	7—4 4—8	1—5 3—7
2—3 4—2	2—3 4—3	6—8 2—6	7—4 2—8
5—6 3—6	5—1 5—6	1—2 3—5	6—8 5—4
3—1 5—1	6—2 3—2	7—5 4—1	1—2 1—7
6—4 3—4	4—5 6—4	4—6 8—7	3—5 3—6
2—5 6—2	1—2 1—3	1—3 5—6	8—7 4—2
1—4	5—3	8—5 3—4	1—3 5—6
		4—2 8—1	4—6 8—1
		1—7 5—2	4—8 7—5
		3—6 6—7	5—2 2—6
		2—8 8—3	6—7 8—3
		5—4 1—5	8—5 4—1
		6—1 7—2	5—6 7—2

*Use these numbers for team mates.

LEGEND

V	—	Victory
D	—	Defeat
HG	—	Hits Given
HR	—	Hits Received
PL	—	Place
IND	—	Indicator

Note: The fencer called first must place himself at the right of the president. If one is left-handed, the fencers position themselves with their chest side to the president.

hits received. For example, if Fencer A scored 15 hits and received 19, A's indicator would be −4. If Fencer B scored 16 hits and received 19, B's indicator would be −3. Fencer B would place higher than Fencer A. On the other hand, Fencer C with 18 hits scored and 16 received would have an indicator of +2 and would place higher than Fencer D with 16 hits scored and 16 received, showing an indicator of 0. *In the case of a tie with equal indicators, the fencer with the lowest number of hits received is placed highest.* In lengthy competitions the indicator obtained in the first round of bouting is ignored in totaling the aggregate of indicators. For a detailed table of indicators, consult the official rules book.

Should there be absolute equality of victories and indicators, the tied competitors fence a barrage. When, in the final pool, there is a tie for first place, the order is determined by barrage.

With the introduction of electrical scoring machines, a somewhat different officiating technique is required since the electrical apparatus replaces the four judges.

The bout is directed by the president, who moves up and down alongside the strip to follow the action while keeping the light signals in view. At the beginning of each bout, and whenever an electrical weapon is changed, the president must check the resistance of the spring in the point by means of a 500-gram weight. The point of the blade contains a spring attachment which, when depressed, breaks an electrical circuit and causes the apparatus to signal a hit. This hit activates a buzzer and a light. If the light is colored (red for one fencer, green for the other), the hit is valid. If the light is white, the hit is invalid. However, the president may declare a hit against the fencer who covers a valid target with an invalid one. An off-target hit (white light) halts the action and nullifies any subsequent action by either fencer until the bout is resumed. For example, if both signal lights (white and colored) appear on the same side of the apparatus, a nonvalid hit has preceded a valid hit. The president's decision in this instance is "no score." On the other hand, the electrical scoring device is so constructed that, when a valid hit is followed by an off-target hit, *only the colored light goes on.*

It must also be noted that the *electrical apparatus does not indicate any priority*

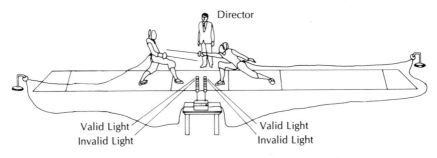

POSITIONING OF DIRECTOR AND ELECTRICAL APPARATUS
(the invalid— off-target—light is used only in foil fencing)

in time between two or more hits which register at approximately the same time. It is the president's function to award the touch by application of the principle of right of way, which gives the fencer who initiates an aggressive action the right of way. An aggressive action is interpreted as the *movement of the weapon* toward the opponent in an attempt to threaten the target.

The fencer so threatened must defend or parry before riposting. The fencer who has parried acquires the right of way. If the riposte is hesitant, the opponent may retake the right of way by resuming the attack. There are some exceptions to this rule. For example, when a compound attack is made and the opponent's stop hit lands before the start of the final movement of the original attack, the counterattack has the right of way. Fencing tempo is not so much a time measure as an action measure. (See Chapter 5 concerning time action, pp. 47, 49.)

The president employs the rule of right of way only when simultaneous or near-simultaneous hits are made. The speed and mobility of modern fencers create situations which may be difficult for novice officials to interpret. However, this rule, when correctly interpreted, will aid officials in establishing the orderly sequence of movements.

A general knowledge of duties and specific techniques will help develop competency in officiating.

The president (director) is responsible for the following:

(a) To make certain the judges, scorekeeper, and timekeeper understand their duties, and that the fencers understand the strip boundaries.
(b) To visually check all fencers approaching the strip for assurance that they are safely outfitted: for example, to detect such hazards as holes in the jacket, long hair draped over any part of the target area, or bare legs.
(c) If electrical equipment is used, to make arrangements for having the fencers hooked up so time is not lost.
(d) To determine the sequence of movements by concentrating on the action of the blades, *not* the target. The target is the *responsibility* of the judges or the electrical apparatus.
(e) To reconstruct only that phrase or portion of a phrase which directly affects the outcome, avoiding verbose reconstructions.
(f) To speak clearly and loudly and to state decisions with certainty.
(g) If an electrical machine is used, to move so that the machine is visible between the contestants at all times.
(h) For the sake of clarity and uniformity, if no hit has been awarded, to announce, "No score!" To avoid other statements such as "Nothing done!"

Judges are responsible for the following:

(a) To move with the action on the strip.
(b) When a hit is observed, valid or invalid, to immediately and vigorously raise a hand high. Not to hesitate.
(c) To respond to the director's question by reporting only what is *seen*, not what is *heard*.

(d) To respond decisively and independently.

(e) To avoid being intimidated by a fencer.

Scorekeepers are responsible for the following:

(a) As soon as a bout is completed, to announce loudly and clearly, "(*Name*) and (*Name*) fencing," "(*Name*) and (*Name*) on-deck." (On-deck means that the two named opponents should be ready to fence next at the conclusion of the current bout).

(b) If the electrical scoring apparatus is not used, to announce the score clearly after each touch: for example, "3–2, against Mr. Jones."

(c) When a pool of bouts has been completed, to indicate on the score sheet the *place* each fencer earned, have the president sign the sheet, then submit it to the tournament chairperson.

Timekeepers are responsible for the following:

(a) Unless otherwise instructed, to time only that interval between the director's commands "Fence!" and "Halt!"

(b) To call "Time!" immediately prior to the start of the last minute. The president will stop the bout and notify the competitors that one minute of fencing time remains.

(c) To call "Time!" loudly or to signal with horn, bell, or whistle at the expiration of the final minute.

Those assigned to electrical-machine operation are responsible for the following:

(a) To make certain the apparatus faces the president.

(b) To wait until the president asks "Ready?" before clearing the machine.

(c) To avoid clearing the machine prematurely.

Officiating in fencing is a difficult task, but it provides a dynamic challenge for those who have the necessary attributes.

LEARNING EXPERIENCE

1. *Attend a fencing tournament in your locale. Carefully observe a capable president. Mentally make your own decisions about the fencing action and compare your decision with that of the expert president.*

2. *Volunteer to keep score or time at a fencing meet. Those in charge will gladly explain the proper procedures. Helping at a meet will familiarize you with tournament procedures and will enable you to observe the fencing and the officiating.*

3. *Use an audiovisual machine to observe yourself directing a bout, and to photograph other fencing situations for study and analysis.*

HIGHLIGHTS

1. List at least six skills and/or personal characteristics required of officials.

2. List the titles of the officials in a conventional bout and explain the duties of each.
3. Explain the difference between "yes," "no," and "abstention" votes by a judge and a president.
4. Given any combination of the above votes by two judges and the president, determine the correct decision.
5. Explain the rule of right of way and how it is employed in officiating.
6. Explain the proper use of a scoresheet.
7. Explain how the number of officials, responsibilities, and techniques used in an electrically scored bout differ from a conventional one.
8. Contact the Amateur Fencers League of America regarding their program for training and certifying directors.

8

Physical Fitness

Concept: Attaining a High Fitness Level Requires a Conditioning Program Designed for Individual Needs.

Conditioning should be a progressive, continuing process in .which the fencer engages several times a week throughout the year; it should not be limited to weekends or concentrated into one or two days. A regular medical examination should be required, with particular emphasis on the individual's capacity to engage in strenuous physical activity (see Chapters 13 and 14 on legal responsibility). The instructor or coach should discuss the medical-examination reports with each fencer (or parent/guardian of a minor), as noted in Chapter 13, and should recommend professional advice regarding potential problems, including excessive weakness or fatigue or abnormal body weight. Good general health habits are essential to conditioning.

Endurance, flexibility, speed and quickness, and agility are the fitness components for achieving satisfaction and success in fencing. They can be developed with a program of exercises and drills. Naturally, the components are interrelated; improvement in any component will be accompanied by improvement in the others. Muscle efficiency will improve with conditioning. "Correct" movements require less energy, result in less fatigue, and are more efficient than are the movements considered incorrect.

The exercises in the Learning Experiences that follow are suggestions for developing certain fitness components and specific body areas. They have proven their usefulness; however, many others can be developed that relate directly to fencing skills. Individual differences such as those of age and general health will necessarily require differing levels of intensity in any conditioning program. The level of intensity (dosage) recommended in the following exercises reflects the level considered necessary for *maintaining* good physical condition *after* an adequate level has been achieved. Beginners should start at a lower level and increase the intensity or the number of repetitions until they can perform at the recommended level. The instructor or coach should set the exercise dosage for each fencer as a recognition of the fencer's readiness for progressively higher competitive levels.

Warm-up Exercises.

Every workout or competition should begin with warm-up exercises designed to stretch the muscles and tendons and to prepare the body for more strenuous activity. The warm-ups should include the following:

neck circumduction (5 to 10 repetitions)
extended arm circling (20 to 30 repetitions)
torso twisting (5 to 10 repetitions)
side bending (5 to 10 repetitions)
opposite-toe touching (10 to 15 repetitions)
half knee bends (5 to 10 repetitions)
sitting hamstring stretcher (3 to 5 repetitions)
Achilles stretcher (3 to 5 repetitions)

LEARNING EXPERIENCE—WARM-UPS

Experiment to discover the point at which a warm-up has loosened your muscles without exhausting you. Feeling "loose" and beginning to perspire are generally signs that you are sufficiently warmed up.

Endurance.

Muscular and cardiorespiratory endurance is necessary for extended competitions. Even a small number of bouts requires endurance if it is composed of lengthy fencing phrases.

Developing endurance and strength requires the application of the "overload principle," which challenges the body *a little more at each session.* Initially the muscles will ache, but the pain will disappear as muscle tone and endurance develop. Merely repeating easy work loads will not build endurance.

Endurance also helps improve the psychological factors of motivation and the will to endure pain and discomfort. In personality development this will is called persistence. No amount of *discussion* will develop this trait; its origin is *mental,* but its attainment is *physical.* A person must *want* to fence!

LEARNING EXPERIENCE—ENDURANCE

1. Jog—walk—jog. *The fencer should check with a physician to determine the recommended maximum heartbeat level for use in monitoring his or her development with this exercise. Then each fencer should establish a jog—walk—jog schedule for optimal benefit.*
   Purpose: *To improve cardiorespiratory fitness.*
   Dosage: *Thirty minutes per session—at least four sessions per week.*
   Variations: *Increase the distance (or time) for each jog until a minimum of two miles can be covered. Alternatives are bench stepping, cycling, rope skipping, distance swimming, and specially designed exercises.*
2. Running continuously. *A more intense training exercise than the jog—walk—jog, providing the activity can be sustained for longer than 10 minutes.*
   Purpose: *To promote cardiorespiratory fitness.*
   Dosage: *11 to 12 minutes per session—at least three sessions per week.*
   Variations: *Distance cycling, rope skipping, distance swimming.*

Flexibility.

With good flexibility the muscle can move efficiently throughout its range, allowing optimal performance with relatively little chance of injury. Flexibility is governed by individual bone structure and soft tissue; bone structure is essentially fixed whereas soft tissue can be stretched. More flexible thigh muscles permit a longer lunge, and a greater reach is possible with more flexible arm and shoulder muscles. Well-toned and flexible muscles do not clutch, grab, or feel tight. Stretching exercises should be performed slowly, and progress should be gradual. Avoid sudden jerky movements that might strain the muscle or tendon.

LEARNING EXPERIENCE—FLEXIBILITY

1. Static stretch. *Move each body or limb segment (individually) through its range of movement until a "pain threshold" is reached; then maintain this stretched position for three seconds. Remember that stretching should be performed slowly, without jerks or bounces that can cause injury. This exercise is best performed along with the daily warm-up exercises.*
2. Trunk flexion. *Sit with legs fully extended and feet together against a bench or board. Extend the arms and slowly stretch toward (or beyond) the board as far as possible, then hold this position for a count of three. Measure the distance between the tips of the fingers and the board—either short of the board or beyond it. Measures beyond the board are plus scores; those short of it are*

minus scores. Effort should be made to gradually increase the extent of the stretch.
Purposes: *To increase trunk flexion and stretch the back muscles and back thigh muscles (hamstrings).*
Dosage: *Five to ten repetitions.*
Variations: *Toe touching, trunk twisting, side stretching.*
3. Trunk extension: *Lie prone (face down) on the floor. A partner should straddle your legs, holding them and buttocks down: Place both hands behind your neck and raise the chest and head off the floor as far as possible. Hold this position for a count of three. Measure the distance from chin to floor.*
Purpose: *To increase the range of backward upper body movement.*
Dosage: *Five to ten repetitions.*
Variation: *Toe touching, trunk twisting, side stretching, butterfly swimming stroke.*
4. Shoulder Lift. *Lie prone (face down). Extend the arms parallel, holding a bar or wand in both hands (palms down) with chin on the floor. Lift the wand and chin as high as possible and hold for a count of three. Measure the distance from shoulder to floor.*
Purpose: *To increase the range of movement of the shoulder girdle and back.*
Dosage: *Five to ten repetitions.*
Variations: *Arm circling, toe touching, trunk twisting, side stretching, shoulder shrugs with weights, shoulder rolls hanging from a bar.*
5. Lunge Stretcher. *Assume a well-balanced lunge position. Place the left hand on the left hip and the right hand on the right knee. Push against the hip, forcing the thigh to stretch as the hip is lowered and the lunge elongates. Maintain this position for 12 seconds. Reverse the leg positions and repeat.*
Purpose: *To stretch the thigh muscles and increase the range of movement.*
Dosage: *Five to ten repetitions.*
Variation: *Stride stretcher—With knees on the floor, place one foot forward so the knee is directly over the heel of the foot. Press the hips downward and forward while keeping both knees stationary. Hold for 30 seconds. This exercise is good for lower back and hip flexibility.*

Strength.

Strength is necessary in the hands and shoulders for holding and manipulating the weapon throughout the bout. The legs must be strong for maintaining body balance, maintaining the fencing stance for long periods, and generating power for driving the body forward quickly with great force. Current research indicates that an increase in muscle-fiber size is a factor in developing strength. The overload principle appears to be most useful in a strength-developing exercise program.

LEARNING EXPERIENCE—STRENGTH

1. Ball squeeze. *Practice squeezing a tennis-size ball, with each hand.*
Purpose: *To increase the strength of the fingers, hand, and forearm.*

Dosage: *Twenty to thirty repetitions with each hand.*

Variations: *Substitute balls with more resistance. Use steel coil-spring exercisers for the same purpose. Periodically check the grip strength with a Stoelting Grip Dynamometer.*

2. Push-ups. *Assume a prone position (face down) with the palms at the shoulder point. Push with the arms until fully extended while keeping the body and legs straight. Flex the arms and lower the chest to the floor. Repeat.*

    Purpose: *To increase the strength and endurance of the arm extensors, the shoulder girdle, and the chest muscles.*

    Dosage: *Twenty-five to thirty repetitions.*

    Variations: *Pull-ups (with palms outward); dips on parallel bars.*

3. Four-count leg exercise. *Lie supine (on the back) with your hands at your side. Raise the legs slowly about 18 inches (45 centimeters). Hold for at least one second. Spread the legs wide and then return. Hold for one second, then lower the legs gently to the floor. Repeat with a slow count.*

    Purpose: *To increase the strength and endurance of the thighs and abdominal muscles.*

    Dosage: *Ten to twenty repetitions.*

    Variations: *Bent-knee sit-ups, flutter kicks, sitting tucks.*

4. Wall sit. *Assume a sitting position with the back against a wall and the knees together. The upper legs should be parallel with the floor and the lower legs should form a right angle at the knee. The buttocks should be knee high. Hold this position.*

    Purpose: *To increase the strength and endurance of the calves and thighs.*

    Dosage: *Twenty seconds to one minute for each repetition. Five or more repetitions.*

    Variations: *Endurance hops, bench stepping, toe risers with weights.*

5. Sit and stand. *Sit back-to-back on the floor with a partner, legs flexed and arms locked. On command, rise together by pressing backs and extending legs. On command, reverse the procedure and return to the sitting position.*

    Purpose: *To increase the strength and endurance of the calves and thighs.*

    Dosage: *Five to ten repetitions.*

    Variations: *Vary the quickness of commands and execution. Endurance hops, bench stepping, half knee bends with weights.*

6. Wrist rotation with weights. *With a five-pound weight in each hand, palms down, extend the arms forward parallel to the floor. Slowly rotate the wrists clockwise for ten repetitions, then repeat counterclockwise. Increase the weights as strength develops.*

    Purpose: *To increase the strength and endurance of wrists, arms, and shoulders.*

    Dosage: *Ten to twenty repetitions.*

    Variations: *Repeat above with palms facing upward; flex the wrists up and down with weights,*

7. Wrist roller with weights. *This apparatus is a bar with a rope or cord at the center, by which a weight may be suspended. Start with a five-pound weight suspended from the bar and reaching the floor from shoulder height. Support this with the arms extended. Rotate the bar forward to lift the weight, using the hands alternately, and winding the rope onto the bar. Reverse the wrist action,*

slowly lowering the weight to the floor.
Purpose: *To increase the strength and endurance of the wrists, arms, and shoulders.*
Dosage: *Start with five repetitions and work up to twenty.*
Variations: *Increase the weight as strength develops. Perform the same exercise with the elbows pressed against the sides.*

Speed and quickness.

Speed and quickness play a vital part in achieving success in fencing. Both overall tempo and reaction time are involved. Increases in strength and flexibility improve speed. The correct learning of skills improves both speed and quickness, as improper or unnecessary movements are eliminated. Warming up the muscles helps them to work more smoothly and quickly.

LEARNING EXPERIENCE—SPEED AND QUICKNESS

1. Squat thrusts. *From a standing position, move to a squat position by bending both knees, and place the hands on the floor about shoulder width apart. With the arms extended, thrust the legs back so the body is straight. Return to the squat position, then return to the standing position. Increase the tempo as ability improves.*
   Purpose: *To strengthen the muscles of the arms, legs, and body.*
   Dosage: *Fifteen to thirty repetitions.*
   Variations: *Alternate striding from the front-leaning rest position, rope skipping, wind sprints.*
2. Drumming. *In the on-guard position, on the balls of the feet, alternately lift each foot from the floor rapidly (similar to running in place). Continue for one minute, rest ten seconds, then repeat five times. Speed should be increased as much as possible while maintaining balance in the on-guard position.*
   Purpose: *To increase the speed of foot and leg movements.*
   Dosage: *Five to ten sets.*
   Variations: *Advance and retreat while drumming.*
3. Pin-the-glove. *The fencer assumes the on-guard position at lunge distance from a wall. A partner releases a glove held against the wall at 2½ meters height. The fencer must lunge and pin the glove against the wall before it reaches the floor. As the fencer's skill improves the glove should be dropped from lower points.*
   Purpose: *To sharpen reaction time and develop quickness.*
   Dosage: *Fifteen to thirty repetitions.*
   Variations: *The glove can be thrown on the wall from a point behind the fencer. The fencer may undertake to prick one balloon or more among three or more placed vertically on the wall.*

Agility.

Not only must fencers move speedily and react quickly, but in addition they must constantly change direction without losing balance. Fencers must be light and bouncy on their feet and able to maneuver their bodies like dancers.

LEARNING EXPERIENCE—AGILITY

1. Thirty-foot agility run. *Station four obstacles, such as chairs, 10 feet apart, with one obstacle placed at the Start-finish line. Start from a prone position near the Start point. On the command "Go," run directly to the 30-foot line and return by the same route to the Start line. Continue to run, zigzagging around the obstacles to and from the 30-foot line. Then upon reaching the Start line sprint to the 30-foot line and return to the Finish-start line.*
   Purpose: *To gain facility in changing direction without losing balance.*
   Dosage: *Until the course can be run successfully at reasonable speed.*
   Variations: *Advancing or retreating in response to signals by the coach/instructor (whistles, hand claps, or gestures). Following a leader through the course while keeping a specified distance.*
2. Burpee (squat thrust) four-count exercise. *Start by standing in the position of attention. On the count of one, assume the squat position and place the hands on the ground. On the count of two, extend both legs to the rear. On the count of three, return to the squat position. On the count of four, resume the original position standing at attention.*
   Purpose: *To gain facility in taking positions from the motionless state.*
   Dosage: *Fifteen to thirty seconds continuously; then repeat until the exercise can be done without loss of balance.*
   Variations: *Competitive games—dodge ball, spud, bombardment dodge ball (using several balls). Competitive relays—sprint baton relay, leapfrog relay, rope-skip relay.*

Highlights

1. List and define the components of fitness required for optimal fencing performance.
2. Define the overload principle and tell what effect it has on fitness.
3. Explain the effect that health habits have on fencing performance.
4. Explain the relationship between warming up and performance.
5. Maintain a personal schedule, in which you record conditioning activities and dosage and note changes in your fitness level.
6. Correlate fencing performances with fitness levels at various times during the year.

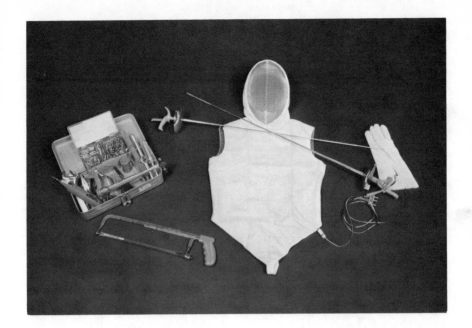

9

Equipment for Competition

Concept: Competition Fencing Demands Supplementary Equipment.

Choice of personal equipment will become more selective as the fencer improves. The individual's choices usually include the weight and balance of the foil, the weight and fit of the uniform, the weight and design of the mask, and the traction and feel of the shoes.

The official uniform includes the full jacket, trousers, shoes, socks (knee socks if knickers are worn), and glove. A white or very light ecru uniform is required for competition. Colored knee socks and trousers with seam stripes may be worn for institutional identification.

When selecting a uniform, consider the quality and type of material (gabardine, duck, stretch, or twill), comfort and ease of movement, and style. A second jacket should be available for long tournaments or if the fencer perspires profusely.

Full jacket. The jacket usually has a double lining in the sleeve, under the armpits, and across the chest. The rules require that women's jackets carry additional padding across the chest, or that a padded vest be worn under the jacket. All fencers are required to wear under the jacket a one-sleeved plastron for the weapon arm. It is held in place by elastic or buttoned straps, and is usually of gabardine, twill, cotton, or synthetic material. Arm patches, if used, are worn only on the sleeve of the rear arm.

Trousers. Trousers are available in various styles—long pantaloons, tapered full-length trousers, or knickers. If knickers are worn, knee socks are necessary for leg protection. Adhesive tape may be used to prevent the socks from sliding down and exposing the legs.

Warm-up trousers and jackets. Warmup clothing is available in a wide variety of styles, fabrics, and colors. It is worn to retain body heat and to prevent chilling between bouts. All Olympic teams, most school teams, and many individuals wear warm-up clothes.

Shoes. Fencing shoes of soft leather have reinforced areas to prevent wear and have treads designed for good traction. Although more expensive, they usually wear longer than regular tennis or gym shoes. Fencers subject to heel bruises may wear a plastic heel cup inside the shoe of the lead foot.

Socks. Socks are available in a variety of fabrics (cotton, wool, nylon, and other) and styles (knee length, medium length, and ankle length). The choice of fabric and style is left to the fencer.

Gloves. Fencing gloves should have a cuff or gauntlet that overlaps the sleeve of the jacket. Those designed for electrical fencing have a hole through which the body cord can emerge.

Electric foil. Electric foil fencing requires each combatant to have an electric foil, a body cord, and a metallic vest. (See Chapter 10 for further details.) Since the electric foil is heavier than the conventional foil, it is advisable to purchase a practice blade of similar weight for training. Most beginners use a French handle; however, if difficulty is experienced in controlling the electric foil, it might be advisable to try an orthopedic handle. Tournament regulations require each fencer to have two operable weapons since mechanical failures sometimes occur during bouts. If it is necessary to borrow equipment, the fencer must assume responsibility for any damage to it.

Body cord. Great care should be exercised in all handling of the body cord, especially when it is being connected to the reel or disconnected from it. During storage or transportation it should not be bent at sharp angles or pinched by tight packing against hard objects.

Metallic vest. The metallic vest worn over the valid target area is covered with lamé fabric that has metallic threads woven into it. Under this is a vinyl lining that acts as a buffer between the metallic cloth and the inevitably perspiration-dampened jacket. Perspiration, frequent hits in an area, and repeated folding can rupture the metallic threads. There is no magic formula to prevent corrosion, holes, or broken wires. However, the metallic garments will last a long time with proper care and attention. It is recommended that they be carried on a hanger in a ventilated plastic bag. They should be aired and dried after any competition. Holes, tears, or dead (nonconducting) spots can be repaired with fresh lamé patches (or swatches). Vests should be washed in lukewarm water with mild soap or detergent ("gentle suds") and hung to dry. Do *not* wring out the garments. All fencing garments should be drip dried.

Mask. The fencing mask must be formed of strong mesh, which should be rustproofed by hot tinning. The wires must have a minimum diameter of 1 millimeter before being tinned and should be spaced no more than 2.1 millimeters apart. The mesh must be insulated inside and out. Masks come in three sizes—small, medium, and large—and are adjusted to fit by changing the shape of the back spring or the head support. The bib and trim must be white.

Tools. Several basic tools are required to maintain equipment. A small pouch or bag can be used for such tools as a screwdriver, pliers, a 500-gram test weight, a small signal tester or ohmmeter, shims, a small portable vise, an Allen wrench, a jeweler's screwdriver, emery paper, electrician's or plastic tape, extra retaining screws, and springs.

All participants in fencing should learn to diagnose troubles in electrical equipment and to repair them, since the working order of personal equipment is the responsibility of each fencer. The director can annul only the last hit made before an equipment fault has been established. Therefore each fencer has the responsibility to watch for any erratic equipment performance and report it immediately. For most problems a procedure can be established that will locate the faulty component in a logical and progressive manner (see Chapter 10).

Weapon bag. A weapon bag is a practical necessity for carrying fencing equipment. Bags of canvas, vinyl, or leather are available in various sizes to satisfy both individual and team needs. It is recommended that clothing, shoes, and gloves be packed in individual plastic bags to be neat and to prevent moisture from affecting the equipment. Bags should be brushed and aired frequently, especially after a heavy workout or a tournament.

LEARNING EXPERIENCE—SUPPLEMENTARY EQUIPMENT

1. Compare the comfort, wearing quality, and washability of fencing uniform materials (gabardine, duck, stretch, twill). Which do you prefer and why?
2. Interview fencers to find reasons why they prefer various trouser styles. Which would you prefer to wear?
3. Practice replacing a spring in the tip of the blade, taping the blade, and replacing the blade.

HIGHLIGHTS

1. List the components of an official fencing uniform.
2. List the items required for electric fencing.
3. Explain the advantages of using an electric foil with an orthopedic handle.
4. Describe how you would care for and maintain your personal gear, including electrical equipment.

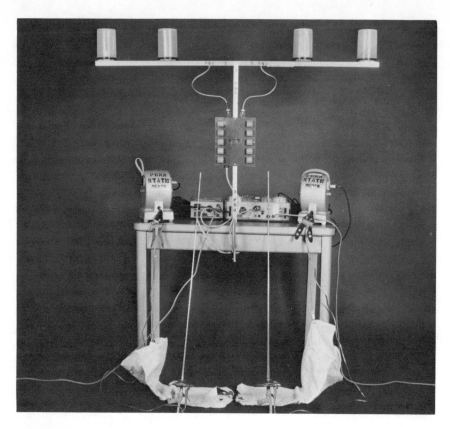

10

Maintaining Electrical Equipment

Concept: The Fencer Must Have a Thorough Understanding of the Electric Foil and the Check Procedures for Insuring Proper Performance.

Officiating and scoring became more efficient and objective with the introduction of electrical foil weapons and recording devices in the 1955 World Championships. The modern recording apparatus has made it possible to serve either foil or épée. In official tournaments the equipment includes:

—a recording (scoring) machine
—extension lights

—two reels
—two floor cables connecting the reels to the recording (scoring) machine
—extension cord to electrical outlet
—metallic piste (strip) which is grounded or neutralized by a cable attachment to
  a reel or the recording machine to prevent touches on the piste (strip) from
  being recorded.

The scoring apparatus for épée requires only two lights (either red or green) to
register touches against either or both fencers. Only in épée fencing can double hits
be scored. The scoring apparatus for foil fencing requires four lights—two (one
white and one colored) representing each fencer. The white lights indicate off-
target or invalid touches while the colored lights represent valid-target touches. If
both lights on the same side go on, it is an indication that an off-target hit preceded
a valid touch. Foil convention would annul the valid hit. If only the one colored
light goes on, the touch would be allowed. If both colored lights go on, the
decision rests with the president (director) of the bout in accordance with foil
conventions and the rule of right of way.

The fencer's electrical equipment includes:
—electric foil (plus at least one additional operating weapon)
—body cord (plus at least one extra cord)
—metallic vest

The metallic vest is designed to cover only the valid-target area, and is worn over
the fencing jacket. The insulated body cord is worn inside the sleeve of the weapon
arm and extends down the back beneath the jacket. One end of the cord is
connected to the electrical weapon socket located inside the foil guard; the other
end of the body cord is connected to a wire mounted in a spring-loaded reel. The
clip on the body cord is then attached to the metallic vest.

The foil is designed electrically as a continuous circuit, and employs a "break"
circuit; that is, the point, when depressed, *opens* a normally closed circuit. The
circuit consists of the insulated wire that begins inside the guard socket, runs along
the groove in the blade, enters the point base, and ends by resting solidly against
the *point pressure spring* in a small insulated cup. (There are two types of foil tips—
see the illustration). The circuit is continued through this spring to the insulated
core of the point. It extends to the point base and back through the blade to the
socket inside the bell guard. When at rest, the point is held forward by the spring.
A touch (tip of the foil touching an opponent with a minimum force of 500 grams)
pushes the point back upon the spring, "breaking" the circuit.

The bell guard is neutralized (or grounded) by means of wiring inside the socket
so a touch on the guard will not register.

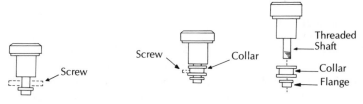

FLANGE-RETENTION STYLE   COLLAR STYLE

A first check should be made in preparation for each competition.

Electric Foils.

Blades. Check for rust, dust, and dirt. Emery cloth or fine sandpaper can remove rust and the like. Be careful not to damage wires.

Tape the front 15 centimeters (about 6 inches) of blade, starting just behind the retaining screws. Tape the foil tip with 1-inch black electrician's tape.

Check spare blades. They should fit handles with the same length of tang and have the same depth of threading.

Check the resistance of the foil circuit. It should not exceed 3.5 ohms with the point at rest. With the point depressed the reading should not exceed 500 ohms. Resistance from any point on the blade and guard to the ground connector of the socket must not exceed 2 ohms.

Foil tips. Check the tip retaining screws. Replace any that are loose or worn.

Check the point travel distance. It must be less than 1 millimeter. If a 1-millimeter shim will fit between the tip and the blade, it will *not* pass inspection.

Check the foil springs. Replace them if necessary. To pass inspection the springs must be strong enough to push up a 500-gram weight.

Inspect the tip for looseness. Tighten with pliers slowly and carefully. Avoid crushing the cylinder housing or stripping the wire insulation.

Guards. Check the diameter of the bell guard. The maximum permitted is 12 centimeters (about 4¾ inches).

Inspect for rust or other stains. Remove them with emery cloth or fine sandpaper.

Check the socket inside the guard. There should be no loose nuts, screws, or bare wire showing.

Inspect the wire-insulating sleeve. The wire must be completely covered by one piece of insulating sleeving from the point where the wire enters the guard to where it is fastened to the socket for the body wire.

Check the condition of the thumb pad. Every electric foil requires a thumb pad to protect the wires from the fingers.

Handles. Check to be sure the handle is properly notched. The notch (half circle) should allow space for the blade wire in its sleeve to pass through without being pinched.

Check the handle insulation. All handles must be insulated. Those not commercially insulated must be covered with insulating tape.

Pommels. Check the pommel fastening. It must be secure. Loose pommels may raise the electrical resistance and cause off-target signals.

All foil-épée pommels for French-handle weapons should be electrically insulated.

Body cords.

For the continental type, check the tightness of the two set screws and the plug springs. Tighten the plug springs by splaying if necessary.

For the twist-lock cord, check to be sure the central screw is tight.

Check all solder joints. Repair them if they are not secure.

Check the crocodile clips for proper functioning. (Mueller No. 27's are recommended.) If the clip is defective, or the spring too weak, it must be replaced. Article 217 specifies the crocodile clip is to be attached "to the back of the metallic jacket on the side of the weapon arm."

Check the resistance at both ends of the body cord. Resistance at either end should not exceed 0.5 ohm.

Metallic vests.

Check the vest for proper fit. It should completely cover the fencer's valid target area.

Inspect the insulating material. If there are any tears or cracks, they must be repaired with insulating tape or replaced.

Thoroughly inspect the metallic threads in the lamé. Pay particular attention to major perspiration areas such as those around the neck and under the armpits. The electrical resistance between any two points on the surface of the lamé may *not* exceed 5 ohms. Any holes, tears, or dead spots can be repaired with lamé patches or swatches. The electrical resistance should be thoroughly checked after patching.

Masks.

Inspect the insulating material. Small tears or cracks may be repaired with insulating tape. If the insulation is damaged extensively, the mask must either be replaced or refurbished.

Check the trim on the mask to be sure it is securely fastened to the mask and that there are no tears or breaks. If necessary, it can be repaired with tape.

Inspect the bib for cracks, tears, or incomplete attachment to the mask. The bib must be attached to the mask so the weapon cannot penetrate between the mask and the bib. Safety demands that the bib be replaced if torn or cracked. A bib should be clean and free from any defects. Rules require the bib to be white.

Check the wire mesh. Be sure the wires are of the proper size and spaced correctly (see Chapter 9). Check to be certain the mesh will withstand the punch test. If the mesh is damaged, or if it fails the punch test, it must be replaced.

A second check should be made at the competition site, just prior to the competition.

Foils and Body Cords.

Using combination foil-épée electrical scoring machines without floor cables and reels. Set the switch to foil.

Hook up two foils to two body cords and plug the cords into the machine. Connect the machine to an electrical outlet and switch the machine to ON.

The pilot light should go on. If any other light goes on, press the reset button. If the machine resets, all is fine. If not, change weapons and/or body cords until machine resets.

Press the foil points against each guard. No lights should go on.

Check for off-target hits by depressing the foil tips singly and together. Use the reset button between touches. Only the white lights should register.

Test for valid hits by pressing the foil tips on the opposite body cord's alligator clip. A valid touch signal (colored light) should register. Test both sides.

Test an off-target hit followed immediately by a valid hit. The white *and* colored lights should go on. Test both sides.

Test for a valid hit followed immediately by an off-target hit. Only the colored light should go on. Test both sides.

If any of the above tests are not fulfilled, the machine is malfunctioning (out of order).

Using machines with floor cables and reels. If the machine is functioning properly, the tests should be repeated with the reels and the floor cables.

Using machines with a metallic strip. If a metallic strip (piste) is being used, depress the foil tip on the piste. If it is properly grounded, no score will register.

A thorough check should be systematically made at the end of the season.

At the end of the season, a complete check, repair, and storage routine should be performed.

Take an inventory of all equipment.

Make all necessary repairs.

Thoroughly clean all equipment.

Prepare for storage by a *light* application of a suitable oil.

Store equipment in a well-ventilated area.

Take care of scoring machines to prevent expensive malfunctions and repairs.

Up to this point nothing has been said about scoring-machine malfunctions. This postponement has been intentional. Of all possible troubles, those originating with the scoring machine are by far the least frequent; and in troubleshooting, it is best to play the percentages. This is not to say that the machines may not have eccentricities. They do, but, for the most part, the malfunctions are easily identifiable.

All machines, transistorized or not, can overheat, with characteristics that might vary from one machine to the next. Illumination of the lights for no apparent reason is one such characteristic. This can be either dim or bright. In either case, disconnecting the machine from its power source when not in use will usually control the situation.

Electromechanical relays can get dirty after several seasons of use or incorrect storage. If this happens, resetting can become almost impossible, and it will be necessary to have the relays cleaned—preferably by a professional.

Machine repair is relatively expensive since it requires the services of a professional. Because of this expense, the following two points are very important: (1) The decision that a machine malfunction exists should be based upon a detailed, careful check (such as that outlined above) to be sure an expense is not incurred unnecessarily; and (2) when the malfunction is identified, its characteristics should be noted as thoroughly as possible. In this way the time required for a professional to service the machine can be kept to the minimum.

LEARNING EXPERIENCE—ELECTRIC FOIL AND CHECK PROCEDURES

1. *Compare different scoring equipment. Which do you prefer and why?*
2. *Compare the continental type (two-prong) and the twist-lock type of body cords. Which do you prefer and why?*
3. *Ask an armorer or a knowledgeable fencer to explain and demonstrate the operation of the electrical fencing apparatus.*

HIGHLIGHTS

1. List the equipment required to host an official electric foil competition.
2. Describe the electrical circuit in foil fencing.
3. Practice repairing any holes, tears, or dead spots on your metallic vest with a lamé patch or swatch. Check the electrical resistance of the metallic vest after patching it.

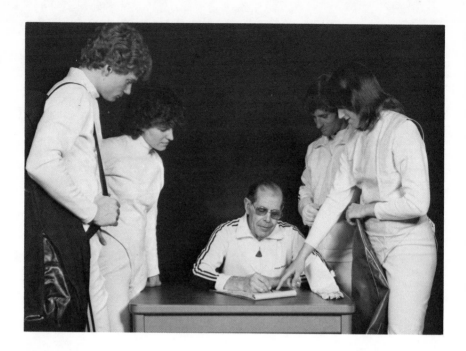

11

Organizing and Conducting Tournaments

Concept: Fencers Should be Prepared to Help Organize and Conduct Fencing Tournaments.

Organizing a tournament is fun, but it does require careful planning. Tournaments obviously differ in size and importance, and they will not all require the same degree of effort. However, *every* tournament does demand attention to detail. In addition to good planning, the smooth conduct of a tournament depends on the full cooperation of organizers, officials, coaches, and competitors. Understanding the problems of organizing and conducting tournaments not only enables the fencer to assist when called upon, but also develops a keen appreciation for the need to adhere to rules and regulations.

Master plan—scheduling.

Two to twelve months in advance. Plan early. Decide on the purpose and type of tournament. List things to be done in writing so an action plan can be drawn up. Clear dates for use of the tournament site. Check school and institution calendars to avoid conflicts. Arrange for directors and possible alternates. Draw up a budget. Order awards. Arrange for public information and publicity. Arrange for necessary equipment so availability will be guaranteed. Organize committees.

One month to six weeks in advance. Organize the tournament and assign duties accompanied by job descriptions. List equipment and materials needed. Arrange for locker, meal, and refreshment facilities. Arrange for overnight accommodations, parking areas, and medical personnel and equipment. Secure scorekeepers, timers, and all other personnel not previously contacted. Draw up a layout for the competition area, including strip locations.

One day to two weeks in advance. Organize the pools for the tournament immediately after all entries are in. Have programs printed and ready for distribution.

The day before the tournament. Set up the registration desk. Review all assignments with personnel. Prepare all facilities and equipment.

The day of the tournament. Start early to recheck the list of things to do. Welcome the participants. Start on time. Be constantly alert to any potential problems during the conduct of the tournament so they can be dealt with expeditiously. Inform news media of the tournament results. Be certain the competition area is cleaned. Check, return, and secure equipment.

The day after the tournament. Evaluate the tournament in writing and file materials which might be of assistance with future tournaments. Write "thank you" notes to all helpful persons and organizations. Send results and photographs to *American Fencing, The Swordmaster,* or other appropriate publications.

For more detailed information on conducting tournaments, consult the *AFLA Fencing Rules* or contact the NFCAA (National Fencing Coaches Association of America). A complete discussion of organizing tournaments is contained in *Tournament Guide for the National Collegiate Championships,* third edition, by M. R. Garret, Candice Corcoran, and Kathleen Russell.

Entry blank—information.

Entry blanks and accompanying material should furnish the participant all the information needed. Specific information should include: the purpose, type, and eligibility requirements of the tournament; the location, date, sponsor, awards, dressing facilities, entry fee, and entry deadline. Travel, overnight lodging, eating accommodations, and ticket information should be included where applicable.

Tournament organization—personnel requirements.

The size of the tournament will determine the division of duties and the number of persons required.

Small tournaments (with 24 or fewer entrants).
Small tournaments would require the following personnel:

Tournament chairman. Determines pools and prepares bout sheets; checks strips, equipment, and supplies; assigns directors, timers, and scorekeepers and lists their duties; makes introductions, announcements, and awards.

Scorekeepers and timers. (See Chapter 7.)

Presidents (directors). Review general rules and ground rules with the fencers; check safety of the equipment and the uniforms; and review judging (if judges are used) and directing techniques.

Bout committee. Acts as a court of appeals and as a resource for interpretation of rules.

Equipment tester. Tests and validates electric weapons, body cords, masks, and metallic vests.

Large tournaments (with 25 or more entrants).

Large tournaments require appropriately larger numbers of the same kind of personnel that small tournaments require for the various duties. In addition, the chairman of the large tournament should consider appointing people to act in the following capacities:

Head scorekeeper. Records scoring information for each fencer on a master scoring chart as well as on the individual scorecards; assigns a scorekeeper for each strip; appoints a captain to assign timers and scorers to the strips for each round and to distribute and collect the scorecards and supplies.

Fencing-area manager. Supervises all arrangements in the fencing area such as placement of mats, tables, and chairs; takes inventory of equipment (including loaned equipment); supervises a crew for dismantling and storing equipment; and takes the responsibility for cleaning the area.

Armorer. Available for repairing electrical apparatus or individual equipment.

Competition area—equipment requirements.

The safety of contestants, officials, and spectators is of primary importance in arranging space. Equipment such as mats and scoring apparatus should be properly set up before the tournament day. Poor organization of the competition area represents a hazard to all concerned and could become an important factor in a potential liability suit.

Minimum floor area per strip. The minimum floor area for each strip should be 17 meters by 5.5 meters (about 56 feet by 18 feet).

Placement of facilities and personnel. The area manager should prepare a scaled plan of the area on a large sheet of paper, marking off areas required for fencing strips, scoring tables, publicity personnel, spectators, and other needs.

Spectators. If the building does not provide suitable separation of spectators and contestants, an area must be set aside for spectators, and should be separated from the contestants by a physical barrier (rope or other) at a suitable distance from any bouting.

Regulation mats. Mats are normally about 6 feet (1.8 meters) wide and 56 to 59 feet (17 to 18 meters) long to allow for at least a five-foot (about 1.5 meters) safety zone at each end. This allows a retreat with slight risk of injury. Markings on the mats should be in accord with the AFLA rules. If mats are not available, masking tape (or other suitable tape) is good for outlining the strips. If the floor tends to be slippery, precautionary measures should be taken to eliminate that potential for injury.

Securing mats to the floor. Every mat (whether rubber or metallic) must be secured to provide firm footing. The sides and ends should be taped to the floor with carpet tape or other strong tape at least four inches wide. Be sure the mats are securely taped to the floor.

Electrical scoring apparatus. Be sure spare machines and spare reels are available.

Scoring and timing tables. A table for scorers, timekeepers, and scoring apparatus should be provided for each strip. Also needed are clipboards, pencils, time clock, whistles, scoresheets, and chairs. Test weights will be needed if electric weapons are used.

Special site arrangements. Certain special arrangements at the site can be of great help in the smooth conduct of a tournament. These include: a designated parking area, a reporting or registration desk to distribute programs and name tags, a practice area, a dressing area and lockers, a lounge area, a refreshment area, storage space, a first-aid area, and good seating for the spectators.

Closing ceremony.

Even though awards are not the primary reasons for holding a tournament, they can and should be symbolic of achievement. These awards can, of course, be purchased; however, the arts and crafts departments of colleges or universities can be used to design them so they will have a particular significance. The ceremony should be dignified and colorful, and it can be impressive. Inviting a well-known personage or school official to make the presentations may enhance the impression. Tournaments can often benefit by the provision of music or some form of entertainment during competition breaks.

LEARNING EXPERIENCE—ORGANIZING TOURNAMENTS

1. *Volunteer your help in organizing and conducting a fencing tournament.*
2. *Write an article for the local newspaper (or magazine) about a tournament in which you have worked or fenced.*
3. *Evaluate a fencing tournament you have organized (or fenced in). Use the following categories as guides:*
   a. *Preliminary planning.*
   b. *Accommodations for teams.*
   c. *Publicity.*
   d. *Competition area.*
   e. *Personnel.*
   f. *Equipment.*
   g. *Ceremony.*
   h. *Follow-up.*
   i. *Safety considerations.*

HIGHLIGHTS

1. List the personnel needed to conduct an interclass tournament.
2. Draw up an appropriate entry-blank form.
3. What information (other than that on the entry form) should be sent to each potential entrant?
4. Design the competition-area layout for five fencing strips and the necessary related equipment, using basketball-court dimensions (typically 50 feet by 94 feet).
5. What considerations should organizers make for convenience and comfort?
6. What safety factors should the tournament organizer keep in mind?

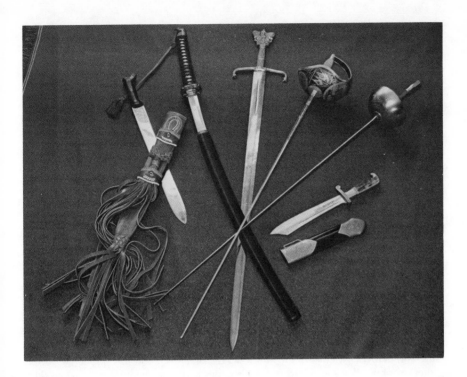

12

Historical and Modern Fencing

Concept: Understanding the History of Fencing Helps Develop a Deeper Appreciation for the Sport.

The sword has played an important role in the history of civilization.

The earliest recorded evidence of a practice fencing bout or tournament can be found in a relief carving in the temple of Madinat Habu, near Luxor in Upper Egypt, built by Rameses III about 1190 B.C. The fencers are shown wearing masks, their weapon points covered, with narrow shields for parrying strapped to their rear arms. Spectators and officials are shown in the background. However, the history of the sword begins at a much earlier date, indeed before written history. From the advent of metal weapons in the Bronze Age, swords were fashioned in many forms.

The copper dagger in use in the Aegean region was followed by the dirk, a longer weapon, which eventually was transformed to the sword.

The swords in the Middle Ages were heavy and clumsy. For many years the two-handed sword was used in combat, heavy armor playing an important defensive role. The styles of fighting were primitive; the strongest arm and the heaviest weapon usually prevailed. With the introduction of gunpowder in the fourteenth century, heavy armor became impractical. Many changes in tactics and weapons quickly followed, transforming swords into lighter, more manageable weapons.

Before 1500, swords were used primarily as slashing/cutting weapons. After 1500, such lighter thrusting weapons as the one-handed rapier became popular. The rapier was used chiefly for attack; defense was entrusted to the rear hand, which carried a dagger, cloak, or buckler. Guilds of fencing masters developed throughout Europe to impart the skills of swordsmanship. Each guild and/or fencing school guarded its tactics and programs from competitors. From the various guilds and schools new fencing techniques developed. Footwork based on geometrical designs was formulated by the Spanish fencing masters. The lunge came into being in the latter half of the sixteenth century. The creation of a single weapon effective for both attack and defense led to the modern fencing positions, which provide a minimum target area to the opponent and give the fencer a longer-reaching lunge. Italian masters in the seventeenth century furthered the development of fencing with the riposte, a counterattacking movement that immediately follows a parry. Other refinements included the introduction of the French foil about 1650, the evolution of the dueling sword in the sixteenth and seventeenth centuries, and the development of the fencing mask for practice in the eighteenth century. Proficiency in the art of fencing became an important attribute and a necessary accomplishment for the nobility and many other members of the leisure class.

With the growth of dueling during the sixteenth and seventeenth centuries, the rapier was replaced by the colichemarde, a thin-bladed weapon, which eventually gave way to the small French court sword. A duel during this era was considered an expression of God's will and was a means for settling disputes. It was not uncommon for armorers and swordsmiths to carve into the blades quotations such as "Trust in God and Me," "Do Not Draw Me Without Reason," "Do Not Sheathe Me Without Honor," or "St. Simon Is My Guide." Faith in divine judgment on the outcome characterized many trials in battle and furthered the chivalric tradition of the Middle Ages. Later, the duel was used to settle legal claims and disputes regarding personal honor. The duel had great impact on fencing as a sport— providing the traditions of courtesy, customs, officiating, and tactics.

The rivalry between the French and Italian schools gave rise to the first international tournaments. Fencing masters from both France and Italy migrated to England, Germany, and other lands where they were well received. In England, King Henry VIII welcomed them and gave his blessing to the sport of fencing, which became a national pastime during the sixteenth, seventeenth, and eighteenth centuries. The French and Italian schools reigned supreme during the seventeenth century. Fencing had developed into a sport with its own rules at the beginning of the nineteenth century.

In the nineteenth century the saber was accepted as the national weapon of Hungary. The French school developed the foil and épée, which, with slight modifications, are the weapons used in competition today. Weapons gradually became lighter and better balanced, resulting in a sport that emphasizes speed of blade and body.

In the last century and a half, the sword has not generally been worn except for military and ceremonial occasions. People may have forgotten the sword's impact on history; however, its influence on dress and custom persists. Buttons on the backs of dress coats are where they once supported a sword belt; ladies take a gentleman's left arm, for earlier gentlemen wanted the right arm free for drawing the sword; and men's coats are buttoned toward the right for ease in opening them with the left hand as the right hand (no longer) reaches for the sword.

The terminology of fencing is extensive and quite different from that used in other sports. Many of the terms used are of French derivation. In fact, the official international language for fencing is French.

Fencing is organized under national and international governing federations.

The Amateur Fencers League of America (AFLA) was founded in 1891 by twenty enthusiasts; the National Fencing Coaches Association of America (NFCAA) was chartered in 1941. Both organizations have promoted interest and participation in fencing among individuals and institutions.

The AFLA is the official governing body for amateur fencing in the United States and is so recognized by the Fédération Internationale d'Escrime, the United States Olympic Committee, and the Amateur Athletic Union. The AFLA cooperates with the National Collegiate Athletic Association, with the Intercollegiate Women's Fencing Association and other intercollegiate groups, and with the National Fencing Coaches Association of America.

The NFCAA membership includes many of the fencing coaches in the country. It is the first coaches' association to have developed an accreditation program leading to a master's certificate.

The United States Academy of Arms was established at the March 1974 annual meeting of the NFCAA. Membership is open to all accredited fencing masters; currently there are approximately eighty in the United States, all of whom are members of the parent organization, the NFCAA. As is stated in the USAA by-laws, this group "resolves to improve, promote and foster the highest quality of fencing and the highest ideals of sportsmanship in competitions with fencing masters all over the world, through defining and establishing the criteria of fencing education in colleges, through setting standards for teaching accreditation, and through acting as an advisory body to amateur groups and associations." For further information about the Academy, correspondence should be directed to the NFCAA office.

Fencing has attracted such a large number of enthusiasts that fencing groups are active in most metropolitan areas and in many smaller cities and towns in the United States. To locate a fencing group, either check with local groups such as the Young Men's and Women's Christian Associations and Young Men's and Women's Hebrew Associations, community centers, recreation departments, high schools, and colleges, or else write to AFLA or NFCAA headquarters. If there is no existing fencing group in your community, one can be organized and sponsored through an established institution.

LEARNING EXPERIENCE—FENCING HISTORY

1. Visit a museum or antique shop and examine the various types of swords and armor used in the past. Compare them with present-day fencing equipment. Note the changes in style, shape, and weight.
2. Watch a historical movie which includes sword fighting and compare that with a modern-day fencing bout. Are the styles historically authentic? List the differences observed.
3. Locate copies of the official AFLA and NFCAA publications. Describe the differences between the two publications.

HIGHLIGHTS

1. List several historical events in the development of modern fencing.
2. Name the governing bodies of fencing in the United States and explain the function of each.
3. Name the local fencing group(s). If none exists, how would you start one?

13

Safety

Concept: Safety Is a Concern of All Persons Engaged in Fencing—Participants, Teachers, Coaches, Officials, Supervisors, and Equipment Manufacturers.

The goals of the following two chapters are:

1. To increase everyone's alertness for fencing safety.
2. To determine everyone's responsibility for fencing safety.
3. To describe safety measures and precautions.
4. To discuss liability and negligence.

According to most definitions, an accident is an unplanned event. An accident might happen to anyone, given certain conditions and/or acts. The undesirable results of an accident in fencing, besides probable injury, may be anger, frustration, and embarrassment for the injured party, plus money costs for medical care and time lost from fencing or other activities. In most instances, medical care for athletes (which may include the services of athletic trainers and use of training supplies and equipment) and the insurance overhead become a cost to the sponsoring institution. The medical and insurance cost to one university supporting 31 varsity teams, including football, was $350,000 for 1979–80. An approximate cost per athlete was $482 since a total of 726 athletes participated that year. The medical and insurance charges allocated to the men's and women's fencing teams (37 fencers) at this institution—on the $482 pro rata basis—amounted to about $17,834. Do you know what this cost is at your institution?

Although medical and insurance expenses are measured in dollars and cents, the fencing instructor or coach is above all concerned with the athlete's well-being. Safety measures practiced by the teacher/coach and the athletes can keep injuries to a minimum. Prevention of accidents, however, is everyone's responsibility. It is the duty of the teacher, the coach, the administrator, the fencer, the medical and maintenance personnel, and everyone connected in one way or another with fencing to be constantly safety conscious.

Before injuries occur, it is the responsibility of the concerned administrators of the institution to see that the instructor/coach, the athletic trainers, and the institutional medical personnel are trained in their roles to provide timely care and service to injured athletes. Every supervisor in the fencing program should be prepared to summon trained medical help from the most appropriate source: the school health service, the team or school physician or trainer, the local emergency operations center or ambulance service. At least one member of the coaching or teaching staff should be qualified to provide initial care while waiting for trained medical help to arrive; specifically, be currently certified in first aid by a recognized agency such as the American Red Cross.

The ability to provide adequate safety measures is a major task for institutions involved in varsity sports and athletic programs. Elimination and/or reduction of injuries becomes everyone's responsibility. Today, every coach and sports instructor must function as a "reasonable and prudent professional" in accordance with the legal interpretation established in law suits involving sports participants who suffered injuries. Care must be taken by the fencing coach/instructor to avoid any hint of negligence on his or her part.

A realistic appraisal of most recent injuries clearly indicates that very few events labeled accidents are really accidents in the sense of being purely chance events. For example, in one collegiate meet a regulation rubber strip (mat) was used. Before the competition began the mat had not been properly cleaned, hence was an unsafe surface for bouting. As a result a fencer tore his hamstring muscle when he lunged. The cause was identifiable, the event foreseeable and preventable. Such unfortunate events occur because people often lack foresight and make mistakes. Consequently, when an "accident" is attributable to "human error" coaches may find themselves being charged with negligence. If the cause of an incident was known to exist, that incident is not an accident. We should not cultivate a philosophy of carelessness and irresponsibility by labeling all unpleasant surprises as "accidents." In some degree we must hold to the belief that administrators, teachers, coaches, officials, and/or participating fencers share in the responsibilities for the mishaps that occur.

Areas of concern in preventing fencing injuries.

Fencing surfaces. The portion of the field of play used for fencing is variously called the strip, the mat, or the piste. The strip may be of rubber, wood, linoleum, cork, artificial turf, plastic, metal, metal mesh, asphalt, or concrete.

The Amateur Fencing League of America *Fencing Rules* require that a host institution must specify to visiting teams the type of surface to be used. The athletes can then select the most appropriate and safest footwear.

If the strip is placed on a platform, regulation prohibits it from being more than 0.5 meter high.

The strip should be extended at each end by 1.5 to 2 meters to allow the fencer crossing the rear limit to retreat over an even and unbroken surface.

All strips should be secured to prevent the mat from shifting, wrinkling, and/or buckling. This may be accomplished by taping the mat to the floor using tape 3 or 4 inches wide (preferably duct tape).

Proper layout of fencing strips in the gymnasium. Fencing requires ample space for mobility, free of obstacles.

The lines of activity should be parallel in order to reduce cross motion and interference with other participants. (See the recommended layouts.)

In tournaments the strips should be so arranged that the fencers and officials have easy access to them.

It is recommended that for each strip there be a minimum floor area, exclusive of passageways or spectator seats, 56 feet (about 17 meters) in length and 18 feet (about 5.5 meters) in width, or approximately 1,008 square feet (about 93.5 square meters) per strip.

The floors and strips should be thoroughly cleaned and dry-mopped as often as necessary.

All fencing areas should be free of all obstructions likely to cause injury or interfere with adequate supervision.

Insufficient space between the side lines of the play area and the walls and bleachers is a common hazard. When such distances cannot be widened, steps should be taken to pad the walls or otherwise eliminate the hazard.

Wherever possible, all fencing strips should be roped off to prevent interference from spectators during the conduct of the bout.

Environmental control factors. The fencing area should be well ventilated and well lighted. Changes in air flow, temperature, or humidity call for adjustments in the body to maintain a body temperature of 98.6° (37°C). The two prime temperature-regulating mechanisms in the body are the sweat glands and the blood vessels. As the environmental temperature nears 80.6°F (27°C) the expansion and contraction of the blood vessels are the primary means of controlling body heat loss through the skin. The unfortunate aspect of having the blood vessels fully dilated is that nearly half of the blood is diverted from the deep body tissue and mental

A RECOMMENDED STRIP LAYOUT FOR A TOURNAMENT IN A GYMNASIUM WITH A RECTANGULAR FLOOR AREA

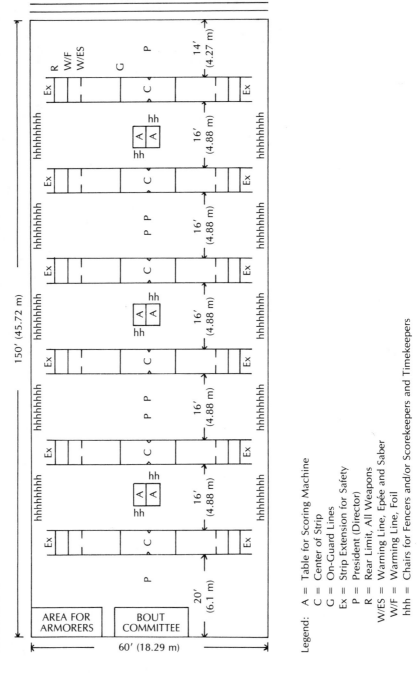

Legend: A = Table for Scoring Machine
C = Center of Strip
G = On-Guard Lines
Ex = Strip Extension for Safety
P = President (Director)
R = Rear Limit, All Weapons
W/ES = Warning Line, Epée and Saber
W/F = Warning Line, Foil
hhh = Chairs for Fencers and/or Scorekeepers and Timekeepers

A RECOMMENDED STRIP LAYOUT FOR A TOURNAMENT IN A GYMNASIUM WITH AN APPROXIMATELY SQUARE FLOOR AREA

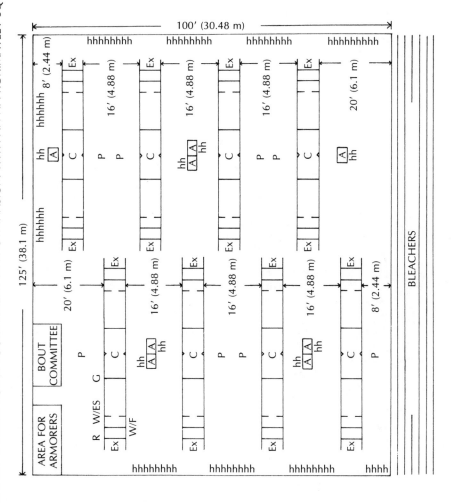

processes to the skin areas and thence straight back to the heart. In consequence, heat stress is a great strain on the heart and our mental functions tend to deteriorate on very hot days.[1]

Owing to the physiological effects of temperature changes on the human body, neither comfort nor maximum efficiency is achieved with excessively high room air temperatures. For an optimum environment with maximum learning efficiency in a practice area, it is recommended that an air temperature of 65° to 68°F (18.3° to 20°C) be maintained.

Factors that could adversely affect visual accuracy should be corrected. Glare control, uniformity of light intensity, and adequate illumination can affect both performance and safety. Prevention of glare is accomplished by use of shields and louvers on light sources and by avoiding high-gloss surface finishes. Uniformity of light intensity refers to the even distribution of lumens across the fencing area to enhance visibility.

"For adequate learning and athletic participation, the main activity area should have 30 to 80 foot-candles of illumination."[2] The instrument used to measure the candlepower of any light source is called a *photometer.*

Selection of fencing equipment.   Proper equipment and supplies are necessary for safe performance by the competitors. Equipment and supplies are usually divided into permanent and expendable categories. *Permanent equipment* is that which usually does not need replacement until after many years of use, such as fencing strips (mats), bleachers, tools, public-address system, scoreboards, and the like. *Expendable equipment* is that which must be replaced regularly because of wear. This category includes fencing masks, uniforms and shoes, weapons and blades, and electronic recording apparatus and reels. The importance of good-quality equipment cannot be overemphasized. The very nature of fencing suggests the element of danger and consequently there is great need for sturdy, safe, and durable equipment. Regular and careful maintenance is extremely important.

Catalogues and price lists can be obtained from the equipment manufacturers and dealers. They are very helpful in comparing quality, prices, and equipment specifications. The addresses for these manufacturers can be obtained from the Amateur Fencers League of America and the National Fencing Coaches Association of America.

Physical preparedness and warm-up.   A teacher or coach assumes final responsibility for the physical preparedness of the fencers. This responsibility is shared with the administration of the institution and with the assigned medical personnel. In order to assure the safest program possible the following steps should be taken:

Require annual medical clearance of all fencers before participating (either in practice or in contests). The medical examination must be made by a licensed

---

[1]Per-Olof Astrand, M.D., and Kaare Rodahl, M.D., *Textbook of Work Physiology,* pp. 491–536 (New York: McGraw-Hill Book Company, 1970).

[2]Kenneth A Penman, *Planning Physical Education and Athletic Facilities in Schools,* pp. 183–184 (New York: John Wiley and Sons, 1977). One foot-candle is equal to one lumen per square foot.

Participant_____ _____ _____
                        (name)   (age)   (sex)

Physical Handicaps   Psychological Handicaps
(Specify missing or injured body   (Specify problem areas such as anxieties,
parts, weaknesses, etc.)   fears, hyperactivity, hypersensitivity.)

bones and joints _____   _____

muscles _____   _____

organs_____   _____

weight problem_____   _____

Chronic Ailments   Allergies
asthma, or other respiratory problems insect bites_____

_____   tetanus shots_____

circulatory or heart problems   other, if significant _____

_____   _____

diabetes or hypoglycemia_____   Blood type _____

epilepsy_____   Current Medication (if any)

hemophilia, or other bleeding problems

_____   _____

Physician Who Conducted Examination

_____ _____ _____
        (name)   (phone no.)   (date of latest examination)

Preferred Personal or Family Physician(s)   Health Insurance (if any)

_____ _____ _____
        (name)   (phone no.)   (name of insuror)

_____ _____ _____
        (name)   (phone no.)   (policy no.)

Parent(s), Guardian(s), or Other Relatives   Employer (if any)

_____ _____ _____
        (name)   (phone no.)   (name)

_____ _____ _____
        (name)   (phone no.)   (phone no.)

_____ _____
        (name)   (phone no.)

A FORM FOR RECORDING MEDICAL INFORMATION ABOUT FENCERS

physician. Records must be maintained for all participants and should include: date and place of physical examination, name of examining physician, kind of examination performed, and listing of medical information in case of emergency. This information should be kept on file and readily available to the instructor/coach. (See the suggested medical-information form.)

Correct remediable defects. Athletes who have remediable defects and who therefore do not pass the medical examination should receive such therapy as is necessary to restore them to good condition. It is the athlete's responsibility to follow through with the prescribed remedial program.

Discuss distinctive physical characteristics and/or medical problems with athletes (or parents/guardians of minors). The instructor or coach should review the medical report with each fencer (and/or parent/guardian) so everyone will fully understand the element of risk resulting from physical and psychological factors. If eyeglasses are required, a mask should be fitted so the glasses can be worn comfortably and so vision will not be hindered. Safety lenses and frames or contact lenses should be required. Allergies, chronic ailments, excessive fatigue or weakness, and abnormal body weight are among other characteristics to be considered. Specialists should be consulted about corrective measures, including improved diet. An instructor or coach should not assume the responsibilities of a physician, trainer, or nutritionist.

Require consent, waiver, and release forms, and keep them on file. "A consent form should be on file for every participant, signed by parent or legal guardian if the participant is a minor, or by the participant. The form should contain a waiver of claims against the sponsor and staff of the program for any aggravation of a pre-existing condition, or for any injury resulting from that condition. The form should also release the program's sponsor and staff from responsibility for any injury occurring during the program. Consent, waiver, and release forms are frequently prescribed by education institutions and athletic associations or clubs. It should be recognized that . . . participant consents *only* to the 'normal' risks of the sport, and that in signing a form does not waive the right to sue for negligence. The supervising instructor/coach should consult a lawyer in case of doubt about the forms."[3]

Develop a testing and evaluation program. The measure of a fencer's physical preparedness is the ability to perform basic skills with *good balance, form, rhythm, technique,* and *endurance.* (See Chapter 8.) Fundamental skills include: (a) stance (on-guard); (b) grasp (grip) of the weapon; (c) hand positions with the weapon; (d) mobility exercises with or without the weapon in hand—advance, retreat, lunge, balestra-lunge, reprise, recovery from the lunge, flèche, and combination of these movements; (e) fencing distance; (f) parries; (g) attacks; and (h) counterattacks.

Mastering these skills prepares a student for the next level—novice competition. A fencer may then progress to higher competitive levels. Progress can be measured by comparative evaluations with other fencers and by performance in competitions.

Athletes should participate in appropriate conditioning (warm-up) exercises before every skill session. All athletes should be thoroughly warmed-up before per-

---

[3]Eugene Wettstone, editor, *Gymnastics Safety Manual,* second edition, pp. 41–42 (University Park, PA: The Pennsylvania State University Press, 1979).

forming strenuously or competing. The warm-up process is different for each individual and is not the same in all weather conditions. A carefully developed warm-up program should be designed to fit each fencer's individual needs.

All athletes should systematically warm-up each major body area before starting skill-training sessions. Suggested exercises may include the following:

head and arms—rubber-ball squeeze, push-ups, pull-ups (chins), dips on parallel bars, flexion and extension of arms with adjustable weights

neck and shoulders—neck rotations, arms swinging, arms crossing, arms and shoulders rotations

feet—ankle rotations, ankle (tendon of Achilles) stretching

legs—stretching thigh and calf muscles using hurdler's position, leg swinging, leg rotations, knee lifting, squatting, walking on tiptoes, walking in a crouch, hopping on both feet forward—backwards—to the left—to the right, straddle hopping, stride hopping, rope skipping, jogging, sprinting

rib cage—trunk twisting, trunk bending, trunk leaning

back—trunk lifts from prone position, leg lifts from prone position, trunk and leg lifts from prone position

abdomen—trunk bending backward, trunk twisting, leg and knee lifts, bicycle exercise from back lying position, sit-ups with knees flexed

lungs—breathing exercises

For other suggestions on this subject see Chapter 8.

Proper progression in the teaching of fencing skills.   The activities and teaching procedures should be organized so the student will pass through a progression of skills as outlined in this book. Particular care should be given to those skill areas involving the greatest incidence of injuries, such as lunging (muscle pulls and/or strains or the like); balestra-lunging, sprinting and running (shin splints, heel bruises, tendonitis); and others of like kind. Just as the success of a team or individual depends upon the acquisition of skills, so does the safety of individuals depend to a great extent upon the mastery of good safety practices. Coaches and teachers should, therefore, be very thorough and meticulous in the instruction of fundamental skills in both fencing *and safety.*

Adequate staff supervision.   All activities, including free or open fencing periods, should be *supervised* by the teaching and/or coaching staff at all times. Liability appears to hinge greatly upon the question of supervision—the degree and character of such supervision as well as the competence of the supervising personnel. Courts have increasingly held that athletic supervisors are responsible for inspection of the environment and equipment. It is the staff's responsibility not only to *supervise the activity* but also to carefully *inspect the area of play* to see that hazardous obstacles are removed and *fencers' protective equipment and gear* are safe. In addition, supervisors should be aware of physiological and psychological stresses that might lead to undue fatigue.

Ratio of teachers/coaches to fencers.   Among the variables that make it difficult to specify a numerical ratio of fencers to teachers/coaches are the ages of the fencers, the methods of teaching, the amount of teaching experience, the skill levels of the fencers, the equipment in use, and the physical characteristics of the instructional facility. However, the authors' personal experience has developed the following guide as a recommendation for the ratio of fencers to teachers/coaches/supervisors in group instruction:

Age of Students	Number of Students per Teacher/Coach/Supervisor
12 and under	5 to 10
13 to 17	10 to 15
18 and over	15 to 25

Development of safety awareness.

The development of safety awareness is fundamental to all areas of responsibility. This includes the establishment of good safety attitudes, a thorough knowledge of the factors involved, and the development of the necessary skills for safe participation.

Attitudes. A safety-conscious attitude in sports is essential if reductions in the frequency and severity of injuries in fencing are to be attained. It should be developed by all persons directly or indirectly involved with the sport of fencing—competitors, coaches, teachers, officials, administrators, equipment manufacturers, maintenance personnel, physicians, athletic trainers, and parents. To inculcate a favorable attitude permitting fencers to enjoy participation in a safe and healthful manner, all of those involved must have an understanding of: (a) factors and conditions that can lead to accidents; (b) principles and practices of accident prevention; and (c) responsibilities of all individuals participating in fencing.

It is essential, too, that the fencer develop the ability to make sound judgments and rational choices with respect to the manner of participation and performance.

Knowledge. Accident prevention in fencing demands a constant awareness of contributing factors—those which are mechanical, physiological, environmental, and psychological, and any others.

Physiological factors include such items as physical condition, fatigue, lack of concentration, or the effects of alcohol or drugs on the athlete.

Environmental factors encompass temperature, humidity, lighting, noise, and physical and architectural barriers.

Psychological factors to consider include emotional reactions to fencing tactics, the attitude and temperament of coaches and competitors, and the atmosphere created by officials in conducting the bout or tournament. The development of courtesy and good sportsmanship is as important as success in competition.

Sound attitudes must be supplemented by knowledge and techniques to counteract hazards, whether physiological, environmental, or psychological. To achieve a significant degree of safety, fencers should be able to recognize, control, and remove hazards, and avoid creating additional hazards.

Skills. Since we tend to enjoy most that which we do *well,* it is essential that the student receive proper instruction in the basic skills with an emphasis on *safety.*

Developing these allows participation in fencing with a high degree of competence, success, and pleasure. Toward this end the instructor/coach should:

(a) Insist on adequate warm-up and conditioning exercises prior to bouting.
(b) Help students develop an awareness of correct general position of the arms and legs in relation to the body when on-guard, in the lunge, in the flèche, or in any of the other varied fencing positions, to prevent bad habits leading to injuries.
(c) Concentrate on having students assume proper posture for all fencing positions.
(d) Teach proper landing of the lead foot when lunging—thereby avoiding heel bruises.
(e) Teach the correct action of the rear leg when recovering from a lunge.
(f) Practice proper footwork (advance, retreat, balestra, lunge, flèche, and their variations), emphasizing balance, rhythm, and sense of distance to avoid hazardous situations leading to injuries.
(g) Establish a sound teaching progression of the fencing skills.
(h) Further the development of the student's tactile, auditory, and visual reactions through simulated competitive drills.
(i) Emphasize the correct response to equipment failure—for example, learn to flex the elbow of the weapon arm immediately upon completion of an attack, especially if the blade breaks.

The Safety Awareness Check List printed here does not pretend to be complete. It is intended as a guide to readers, who are encouraged to make any appropriate additions they deem necessary.

CHECK LIST—SAFETY AWARENESS

Environment:

1. *Is the strip (mat) secure, clean, and safe for instruction and performance?*
2. *Is the fencing area free of obstructions?*
3. *Is the protective equipment—masks, fencing jackets, gloves, underarm protectors—in good condition for the participants' safety?*
4. *Are the weapons safe for use?*
5. *Is there adequate lighting?*
6. *Is the room temperature set at a level comfortable and safe for the participants?*

Individual:

1. *Is the fencer in good health?*
2. *Is the fencer prepared physically and mentally for instruction in a new skill? Balance? Flexibility? Endurance? Coordination? Warm-up? Strength? Motivation?*
3. *Has the fencer any fear or anxiety that may interfere with the safe performance of the skill?*
4. *Has the fencer attained sufficient mastery of the required subskills?*

Instructor:

1. *Is the instructor competently prepared and does he/she have sufficient knowledge of the mechanics of the skill to be learned?*
2. *Is the instructor aware of the individual differences and of the learning sequence to meet each fencer's needs?*

3. *Is the instructor able to make adjustments in teaching strategy to accommodate each fencer's individual level of achievement?*
4. *Is the instructor capable of analyzing the errors in a fencer's performance and making the necessary adjustments or corrections?*
5. *Is the instructor capable of helping slower learners by reducing skills into more basic and meaningful steps?*

A great deal of responsibility is involved in preparing an athlete properly in a safe environment, disciplining the individual to perform skills safely, developing sound and wholesome acceptable attitudes, and understanding the factors that cause accidents or injuries. To achieve a significant degree of safety, the fencers, teachers, and coaches should be able to recognize, control, and avoid creating hazards.

Fencing safety is everyone's responsibility.

Fencing rules.

1. Do not fence without all of the required protective equipment.
2. Use proper conditioning and warm-up exercises before beginning vigorous workout or competition.
3. Check the strip, the electrical equipment, and the area for hazardous or unsafe conditions.
4. Practice and compete only under qualified supervision; check with the instructor/coach.
5. Adhere to established rules and regulations of the Fédération Internationale d'Escrime.
6. Refrain from and prohibit theatricals or horseplay in practice or competitive areas.

Enforcement of safety measures.

The Fédération Internationale d'Escrime (FIE) has developed rules for fencing which also provide safety procedures for those involved. These are set forth in *Fencing Rules—Authorized English Translation of the International (FIE) Rules.*[4] It is mandatory that everyone concerned with fencing (coaches, instructors, officials, manufacturers, and fencers) be thoroughly familiar with these rules. Individual fencers should be particularly concerned with those rules pertaining to personal equipment and clothing (also see Chapter 2).

It is the responsibility of the instructor/coach and the individual fencer to adhere to the rules designed for the performer's safety, and it is the responsibility of the officials to check each fencer and to enforce these safety standards before any bout begins.

[4]Translated by Joseph A. Byrnes (New York: Amateur Fencers League of America, Inc., 1974).

Training of qualified experts.

A major function of the National Fencing Coaches Association of America (NFCAA) has been to upgrade the instructional competencies by *certifying and accrediting fencing masters, prevosts, and instructors.* The United States Academy of Arms, an affiliate of the National Fencing Coaches Association of America, is the accreditation body for those coaches and teachers who wish to be rated as fencing instructor (in one weapon), prevost (in all three weapons), or fencing master (in all three weapons). The examinations for each diploma comprise:

1. *Instructor:* taking and giving lessons; conducting a group lesson; directing; fencing. No written examination.
2. *Prevost* and *Master:* written, oral, and practical examinations. Those interested in applying for accreditation can do so by writing to the United States Academy of Arms, Accreditation Committee, in care of the National Fencing Coaches Association of America.

Certification of officials is an ongoing program sponsored by the Amateur Fencers League of America (AFLA). The Fencing Officials Commission appointed by the Amateur Fencers League of America is the official body designated to develop trained directors (presidents). This program is accomplished by means of clinics, seminars, demonstrations, and other similar means. The Commission also establishes the standards and criteria for the certification of such officials. Candidates who wish to become directors must pass both written and practical examinations. The practical examination takes account of four criteria: mechanics, decisiveness, poise, and analysis of fencing actions. Those seeking Class 3 director's ranking should be prepared to officiate in the French language if seeking an international rating.

Anyone wishing to apply for an official's rating can do so by writing or calling the national or local office of the Amateur Fencers League of America.

Organization and policy.

There is a significant trend involving all those concerned with fencing toward emphasizing the prevention of accidents. This is evident in the growing attention to:

1. Safety education.
2. Licensing, certification, and registration programs for fencing masters and officials.
3. Enforcement of fencing rules and regulations.
4. Thorough conditioning programs.
5. Proper environment and equipment.
6. The importance of "progression" in skill development.

Those who administer sports programs should regard safety as fundamental to their part in a cooperative relationship with all personnel.

Establishing a policy committee concerned with safety is an effective way to educate and motivate personnel. It is a fine method for developing cooperation, exchanging ideas, and developing good safety attitudes, practices, and knowledge.

There are various ways to organize such a committee. A typical structure is illustrated.

┌──── ADMINISTRATOR (CHAIRPERSON) ────┐

MEMBERSHIP	AGENDA

Business Manager
Equipment Supervisor
Grounds Maintenance
    Supervisor
Head Coaches
Head Trainer
Team Physician
	Accident Report, with Charts
	Safety Standing, with Charts
	Lost Time from Classes, Practices,
	    and Competitions Due to Accidents
	    or Injuries Report, with Charts
	Establishment of Safety Practices
	    and Policies
	New Assignments

SAFETY POLICY COMMITTEE—MEMBERSHIP AND AGENDA

Safety indoctrination. It is absolutely essential that a *safety indoctrination program* be held for all beginning fencers. It should stress the importance of avoiding self-caused injuries due to unsafe protective equipment or lack of proper conditioning and of preventing possible injury to opponents because of unsportsmanlike or illegal fencing tactics and unskilled practices. Failure to take proper precautions might result in injury to either fencer, and could entangle both in a negligence law suit. In any event, it is poor consolation to a hurt fencer to think there might be a legal claim against someone else. Quite apart from the legal liability involved, it is morally disagreeable to realize your opponent has sustained a serious injury due to your negligence.

LEARNING EXPERIENCE

1. *Attend a fencing tournament. Carefully note the safety precautions taken or disregarded by the presidents on each strip.*
2. *List the safety measures you take in training and in competition.*
3. *Indicate the safety procedures you would follow if a serious accident were to occur where you practice.*

HIGHLIGHTS

1. Define the term "accident."
2. List those individuals who have a responsibility to see that mishaps do not occur.
3. Design the layout of your gymnasium for a tournament of thirty-six fencers.
4. Perform a check of equipment in your program to insure that safety standards are met.
5. Check with your trainer and/or physician on the number and type of fencing injuries they treat.

14

Liability and Negligence

By Steve Sobel, Counsel,
Amateur Fencers League of America

Concept: Avoid Injuries—Avoid Lawsuits.

The practical approach to legal responsibility is to stay out of court. To do this requires careful planning, the exercise of reasonable care, a knowledge of the law, and an understanding of the risks involved.

Anyone can sue anybody for anything. Therefore, there is no way to completely eliminate the possibility of a lawsuit. Once you are sued, you are a loser. Even if you win the case and are not liable to pay damages to the plaintiff, the victory will be pyrrhic, earned after years of litigation, hours of preparation, adverse publicity, and thousands of dollars in legal fees and disbursements.

The effect of legal fees and litigation costs—the tail wags the dog.

It is costly to sue or be sued, but there is one major difference. Defense attorneys earn their fees whether they win or lose. The plaintiff's attorney is usually retained for a contingent fee. He earns a percent only of the money collected, nothing if he loses. This distinction creates peculiar economic conclusions apart from the merits of any case.

A lawsuit will usually not be started unless there is a good chance to win and collect a large award. Once it is started, everyone remotely involved will be sued since the cost to join additional defendants is relatively insignificant, and bringing them in substantially increases the probability of success. One major injury in sports can therefore result in a million-dollar lawsuit against the opponent, coach, official, owner of the gymnasium or athletic facility, sponsor of the tournament, equipment manufacturers, physicians, and trainers who render aid at the scene. As a potential defendant, your chance of being sued decreases if the injuries suffered are minor or if the liability is questionable.

Every case has a nuisance value for purposes of settlement. It is cheaper for a defendant not to contest a claim if he can pay the plaintiff anything less than the cost of defending the lawsuit, since this cost has to be paid anyway, and payment avoids the risk of losing the case. The plaintiff is encouraged to settle since there is always the possibility of losing everything, and even if the plaintiff wins, he can face years of paying out money he doesn't have for the legal costs of the trial and appeal and for the medical costs of treatment. Pretrial tactics often involve increasing the cost and inconvenience to the adversary by court motions, depositions, and expensive discovery procedures in the hope of achieving an economic surrender of the party least able to afford the costs.

Avoiding litigation therefore involves two basic concepts: minimizing the risk and expense of being sued, and exercising the standard of care necessary to avoid liability.

Minimize the risk and expense of being sued.

Liability insurance.   The most effective method for avoiding litigation expense is to carry liability insurance, since it pays the expense of the litigation as well as any damages awarded. Ironically, it may increase the risk of being sued because it guarantees that money will be available to pay any judgment award. Nevertheless, if this coverage is available at a reasonable cost, be sure to have it. If you don't have specific insurance, inquire how you can be covered. Sometimes coverage is possible by paying a small additional premium on an existing multiperil or umbrella policy. Sometimes organizations offer coverage to members and it can be obtained for a very low premium. Many physical education instructors may be eligible for coverage with the American Alliance for Health, Physical Education and Recreation (AAHPER), or the National Recreation and Park Association (NRPA). Often an employer, university, or sponsor of a particular program may have a policy that will cover the risk. Look into all possibilities and apply for the best coverage available at the most reasonable price.

Waiver of liability.   Parents and institutions involved in the sponsoring and operation of fencing programs will be wise to require participants, and their parents/guardians if they are minors, to sign a waiver of liability form, which should include risks connected with team travel and emergency medical care as well as injuries incurred during participation. These waivers are not absolute defenses since many courts hold them unenforceable for a variety of legal reasons, but there is nothing to lose by obtaining them. It can do no harm, and it often discourages people from bringing lawsuits.

Public relations.   Do not underestimate the value of good public relations as an effective precaution to avoid a law suit. Demonstrate legitimate concern for the athletes, and provide prompt attention when an injury occurs. This practice might prevent those law suits which are started by angry litigants, not for the purpose of obtaining reimbursement damages but to avenge a presumed injustice or insult.

Avoid liability by the exercise of reasonable care.

Liability is based on negligence, which is the failure to exercise reasonable and prudent care. It must be noted that the fencing instructor/coach *must* act as a reasonable and prudent *professional*. Whether this obligation was performed is usually a jury question based on the facts of each particular case. Since two different juries can reach opposite decisions on the same facts, there is always uncertainty. Nevertheless there are general guidelines that have emerged from previous cases which are worthy of careful consideration.

The preceding chapter of this book provides an excellent factual analysis of what constitutes safety in fencing—appropriate fencing surfaces, proper layout of strips in the gymnasium, equipment that complies with FIE safety rules, competent supervision, and adequate emergency care. The discussion in this chapter will therefore emphasize the legal analysis of the qualification "reasonable" as it pertains to these facts.

Competent supervision.   Competent personnel must be in charge, and they must exercise the control and supervision required. The more inexperienced the student, the greater the required supervision. An official at a tournament may be negligent by permitting fencing in his or her presence without the use of safety equipment required by the rules. A coach or teacher has a greater responsibility—to instruct and inform the students, and to require that immature or inexperienced pupils fence only if they can be observed and supervised by trained instructors.

Let's study a few specific examples:

Is it necessary to supervise students while they are warming up? At intercollegiate matches, the coach usually observes the bouts in progress while the on-deck fencers often warm up without supervision, sometimes in another room. Since college varsity fencers are mature individuals who have received instructions on the proper safety practices and acceptable warm-up methods, and since this described practice happens to be common, a coach who permits it is probably exercising reasonable care under the circumstances. At the high-school level and among inexperienced or immature fencers, a trained supervisor should be in attendance. Not that all high-school varsity fencers are immature or inexperienced. Many high-school students are mature individuals and are world-class fencers winning national championships and competing on international teams. However, since the common practice is for local boards of education to require supervision, the failure to supervise creates an issue supporting a jury's finding of negligence. It is therefore wiser to follow the established standard instead of creating your own.

Should coaches give lessons to students not wearing masks and jackets? I have insulted the pride of some coaches by absolutely prohibiting all warm-up lessons at AFLA competitions unless both the coach and student wear a mask and jacket. It is my opinion that lessons without proper equipment are unnecessary, unwise, and unsafe at all times. The AFLA cannot enforce proper safety practices at private clubs. At AFLA competitions, no fencing or lessons are permitted unless proper equipment is worn, and I strongly recommend this standard wherever fencing takes place.

Should a fencer compete after an injury? Who is responsible for making this decision? The supervisor must always exercise reasonable care, and is therefore responsible for the decision. However, decisions requiring expertise which supervisors do not have should be based on the opinions of experts. Fencers should be required to get competent medical advice and submit a written report from their physicians concerning their complete recovery from any prior serious injury or illness. At a competition or practice, someone with adequate emergency and first-aid training and planned emergency access to medical assistance should be available. The supervisor must determine whether a trainer is adequate or a physician is required, which will depend on the nature of the accident and the facts of the particular case.

The important lesson to be learned from the above illustrations is that you must make safety decisions regularly. What constitutes reasonable and prudent professional care is not always clear, and if an injury results there will be many Sunday morning critics reviewing your decision. If in doubt, it is better to be cautious than sorry. Your primary purpose is to avoid injuries and lawsuits, not to exercise the mere minimum care necessary to win a case.

Put safety instructions in writing.   All safety instructions should be in writing and distributed to the fencers for two reasons. First, in the event someone did not hear or understand the instructions, the written material serves as repetition or clarification. Second, the written document is evidence that safety instructions were provided to the participants in the program. If written safety instructions are violated, the individual is then at fault for failure to follow them, but without the written document the violation is difficult to prove.

Safe equipment.   Reasonable care requires the use of equipment that complies with the rules. Underarm protectors, masks, and jackets must be in good condition. Throw out old and frayed masks and jackets. The cost of one lawsuit could pay for all the replacement equipment you would ever plan to buy. (See Chapters 2, 9, 13.)

Safe facilities.   Reasonable care requires adequate space, lighting, and security. Fencing strips should be of satisfactory material, not too close to each other, and not too close to dangerous obstructions such as pillars, doorways, or windows. (See Chapter 13.)

Student-athlete responsibility.   Student athletes should be made constantly aware of the relationship between fencing procedures and safety rules and likewise of their shared responsibility in protecting themselves, their teammates, and their opponents.

Access to emergency care.   The difference between an injury being minor or major often depends on the emergency care rendered at the scene. Advance planning must include knowledge of appropriate emergency procedures, the availability of trained personnel, and the immediate access to essential first-aid equipment. Emergency procedures should be routinely practiced, as are fire drills. (See Chapter 13.)

Conclusions.

The primary purpose of this chapter has been to present *general* advice in the legal aspects of planning a fencing program. Therefore, specific legal theories available as defenses to lawsuits but not pertinent to the planning of a program—such as statutes of limitation, assumption of the risk, proximate cause, and contributory negligence—were considered beyond the scope of the chapter and have not been discussed.

A general discussion of this type is not a substitute for specific advice. You should consult attorneys, physicians, and insurance agents, as well as experienced fencers and coaches. If you need technical advice on fencing, or the recommendation of competent personnel, this information is available at no charge from the Amateur Fencers League of America (AFLA) or the National Fencing Coaches Association of America (NFCAA). Advice is available for the asking; do not neglect to ask.

The proliferation of consumer litigation against professionals for malpractice, against manufacturers for product liability, and against anyone for negligence places everyone in a very precarious position. Although you have no obligation to volunteer, once you do so you must exercise reasonable care. This means you must plan ahead, act carefully, and seek advice in order to make correct decisions that are reasonable according to the facts of each case. Your emphasis should be to plan a safe fencing program for everyone to enjoy. By achieving this, you will also avoid injuries—and lawsuits, at the same time.

LEARNING EXPERIENCE

1. Are you personally covered by health and accident insurance? What is the extent of your insurance coverage? Are others covered by your policy?
2. Does your institution provide for liability, health, and/or accident insurance? What is the extent of this coverage?
3. What safety procedures do you follow when taking a lesson?
4. Study the waiver-of-liability form used at your institution. Do you believe it is comprehensive and informative?

HIGHLIGHTS

1. List the two basic concepts for avoiding litigation.
2. Define negligence.
3. Prepare a poster listing safety rules and regulations to be observed in your practice and competition areas.

Sources of Fencing Information

Books and magazines.

Alaux, Michel. *Modern Fencing.* New York: Charles Scribner's Sons, 1975. This contribution to the fencing library was written by the late Michel Alaux, former United States Olympic coach. In addition to a precise discussion of the techniques of foil, saber, and épée, Alaux offers an analysis of most techniques and elements of fencing, highlighting the salient points. There are excellent photographs and an interesting account of an eighteenth-century fencing master. This is an excellent book for all fencers and instructors.

Amateur Fencers League of America. *Fencing Rules,* 1974 edition. Authorized English translation of the rules of the Fédération Internationale d'Escrime. Translated by Joseph Byrnes. New York: Published by the League, 1974. The 1974 edition of the AFLA manual includes rule changes and additions made by the FIE since 1970. Included is a section on NCAA rules. Competitive fencers should have the latest edition. The book includes: the general rules of foil, épée, and saber; rules for the organization of competitions; disciplinary rules; and articles on equipment.

American Fencing. Published bimonthly by the Amateur Fencers League of America (AFLA). The official publication of the AFLA, this magazine informs fencers of tournament schedules and results and of rule changes and interpretations. It also publishes topics of current interest. For information, write to: Mary Huddleson, Editor, 2201 Bywood Drive, Oakland, California 94602.

Bernhard, Frederica, and Vernon Edwards. *How to Fence.* Dubuque, Iowa: William C. Brown Co., 1956. A loose-leaf book containing 18 fencing lessons, each of which includes a definition of a specific skill, points to be watched in execution, and exercises to reinforce the skill. It also includes a section on history and one on games and festivities.

Bower, Muriel, and Torao Mori. *Fencing.* Dubuque, Iowa: William C. Brown Co., 1966. A great deal of information is presented in this 72-page book. It is written as a supplement for a beginning fencing class and as a review of fencing history, techniques, rules, and bouting.

Castello, Hugo, and James Castello. *Fencing.* New York: Ronald Press, 1962. Emphasis is on the fundamentals of foil fencing "through theory and instruction in fundamental moves . . . practice drills . . . practice bouts . . . and the competitive bout." Especially helpful are the "points to remember" following the presentation of each skill. Of particular interest are sections on conditioning and electric foil fencing.

Crosnier, Roger. *Fencing with the Electric Foil.* New York: A. S. Barnes and Co., 1961. Discusses the effects of electric foil fencing as related to basic movements, the hit, attacks and defense, counter moves, renewals, and presiding.

Crosnier, Roger. *Fencing with Foil.* London: Faber and Faber, 1951. Presents a detailed and comprehensive analysis of skills and techniques and explains the tactical situation in which each skill can be used. The competitive fencer will find the sections on fighting and fighting techniques particularly helpful.

Crosnier, Roger. *Know the Game—Fencing*. London: Educational Productions Ltd., 1952 (Amateur Fencing Association). A comprehensive and compact presentation of the basic skills and equipment required to fence and officiate in foil, épée, and saber.

de Beaumont, C.-L. *Fencing—Ancient Art and Modern Sport*. New York: A. S. Barnes and Co., Inc., 1960. A comprehensive textbook for the modern foil, saber, and épée fencer, whether novice or expert. There are also chapters on tactics, training, judging and presiding, the organization of a fencing club, and the grand salute.

de Beaumont, C.-L., and Roger Crosnier, eds. *Fencing Techniques in Pictures*. New York: Macmillan Co., 1955. Photographs and sketches depicting fencing skills, with concise explanations presented "to confirm instruction received." Each fencing movement is photographed or sketched in four or five phases showing components of the movements. Of the 95 pages, 60 are devoted to foil, the remainder to épée and saber.

de Capriles, M. A., M. R. Garret, and S. S. Sieja. *Tournament Guide for the National Collegiate Fencing Championships*. A guide to assist host institutions and personnel in organizing major tournaments. Current is the 2nd edition; New York: NFCAA, 1975. Forthcoming edition: *see* Garret, Corcoran, and Russell, 1980.

Deladrier, Clovis. *Modern Fencing*. Annapolis: United States Naval Institute, 1948. Mr. Deladrier covers the use of the three weapons from a modern or eclectic viewpont. Of special help to foil fencers is the series of exercises for those clubs and organizations not having a fencing master.

Garret, Maxwell R. *Fencing Instructor's Guide*. Chicago: The Athletic Institute, 1960. To be used in conjunction with or independent of the slide film, *Beginning Fencing*, this booklet provides instruction in officiating, scoring, teaching methods, conditioning, and safety.

Garret, Maxwell R. *How to Improve Your Fencing*. Chicago: The Athletic Institute, 1959. By means of photographs and narration, the author covers the basic skills of fencing, elementary offense and defense, and strategy and tactics. The book serves either as an introduction to fencing or as a review of basic fundamentals.

Garret, M. R., Candice Corcoran, and Kathleen Russell. *Tournament Guide for the National Collegiate Fencing Championships*, third edition. Kansas City: NCAA, 1980. (Forthcoming.) A guide to assist host institutions and personnel in organizing major tournaments. The authors of the first and second editions were M. A. de Capriles, M. R. Garret, and S. S. Sieja.

Hayden, Rob, and Sheldon Berman. *Introductory Foil—A Manual for Instructors*. The Maine Division of the Amateur Fencers League of America, 1978. Available through the national office of the AFLA. This manual presents a series of 16 lesson plans designed for the instructor or high-school coach, but useful to those with considerable experience. An extensive appendix gives additional information on history, basic drills, correcting specific mistakes, footwork, warm-up exercises, infractions and penalties, and club workouts.

Lukovich, Istvan. *Electric Foil Fencing.* Budapest, Hungary: Corvina Press, 1971. Available through fencing equipment companies in the United States. A narrative discussion of the interrelationships of foil fencing components. Lukovich blends the old and new with particular emphasis on the maneuvers and techniques initiated by electric fencing. An appealing book.

Moody, Dorothy L., and Barbara J. Hoepner. *Modern Foil Fencing—Fun and Fundamentals.* Oakland, California: B&D Publications (6645 Heather Ridge Way, Oakland, California 94611), 1972. A loose-leaf book geared to the teacher and/or coach. An educationally sound and logically arranged text stressing fun and fundamentals, well illustrated with stick-figure drawings.

Nadi, Aldo. *On Fencing.* New York: G. P. Putnam's Sons, 1943. Nadi is considered to have been one of the greatest fencers of all times. In this book, he shares with all fencers the finest details of his skill. Chapters on competition, in-fighting, precombat, and combat training are especially fascinating and instructive. Although the book is out of print it may be in libraries, and with persistence it may be possible to secure a copy.

The National Association for Girls and Women in Sports Guide. *Archery—Fencing.* Washington, D.C.: American Association for Health, Physical Education, and Recreation. Published biennially; approximately 35 pages devoted to fencing. Each issue includes the rules of fencing, brief articles on teaching techniques and organization, and a bibliography.

Nelson, Marvin. *Winning Fencing.* Chicago: Henry Regnery Co., 1975. This paperback book is a basic source of instruction for both beginners and developing foil fencers, with brief chapters on épée and saber. Of special interest is the technical vocabulary appendix.

Palffy-Alpar, Julius. *Sword and Masque.* Philadelphia: F. A. Davis Co., 1967. The skills for épée, foil, and saber are clearly described. A spirit of discipline and sportsmanship pervades the book. This is one of the few books containing a section on theatrical fencing. Also of interest are the sections devoted to the history of fencing; training, conditioning, and diet; and the listing of Olympic and World Champions.

Selberg, Charles A. *Foil.* Reading, Mass.: Addison-Wesley Publishing Co., 1976. A comprehensive paperback book for teachers and students alike, with special emphasis on "tactics and the psychological elements of competitive fencing."

Simonian, Charles. *Fencing Fundamentals.* Columbus, Ohio: Charles E. Merrill Publishing Co., 1968. A brief discussion of fundamentals. Techniques are covered from the standpoint of definition, use, execution, common faults, and drills.

The Swordmaster. National Fencing Coaches Association of America, 279 E. Northfield Road, Livingston, N.J. 07039. Official publication of the NFCAA, published four times a year; contains scholarly articles of interest.

Vince, Joseph. *Fencing.* New York: Ronald Press, 1962. For many years Mr. Vince taught fencing to Hollywood stars. In this book he shares his experiences in the development of foil, épée, and saber fencers. An explanation of each skill is followed by a discussion of common mistakes and their causes.

Considerable emphasis is placed on fencing distance. The suggested fencing drills are excellent.

Wyrick, Waneen. *Foil Fencing.* Philadelphia: W. B. Saunders Co., 1971. Contains descriptions and helpful hints of the nature, value, and purpose of fencing, purchase and care of equipment, and movement fundamentals.

Visual media.

(Annotations of visual media are taken from *American Fencing* (Vol. 19, No. 4, March, 1968, p. 18), official publication of the Amateur Fencers League of America. Addresses have been up-dated.

Basic Training of Foil Fencing. 16mm black and white sound film made by master fencers and Olympic coaches from Hungary. Excellent presentation of foil fundamentals from on-guard position, illustrating advance, lunge, fencing distances, parries, and ripostes. Available by purchase or rental from the University of California, Extension Film Center, 2223 Fulton Street, Berkeley, California 94720.

Beginning Fencing. 35mm foil film strips in color with accompanying sound records by Professor Maxwell Garret of The Pennsylvania State University. Contains excellent data on offense, defense, strategy, and tactics. Also available are related explanatory books: *How to Improve Your Fencing* and *Fencing Instructor's Guide.* Available by purchase or rental from The Athletic Institute, 200 N. Castlewood Drive, North Palm Beach, Florida 33408.

Fencing. A complete series of excellent loop films in standard 8mm and Super 8mm, in regular and slow motion with freeze frames. Featured as instructors are Michel Alaux, 1968 United States Olympic Foil Coach, and Csaba Elthes, 1968 U.S. Olympic Saber Coach. Maxwell Garret served as consultant. The loops demonstrate arm and leg technique, simple foil attacks, defense, simple attacks on the blade, compound attacks and compound ripostes, individual fencing lesson employing false attacks, and techniques of saber. Available for purchase or rental from The Athletic Institute, 200 N. Castlewood Drive, North Palm Beach, Florida 33408.

Fencing—Olympics. For information on current Olympic fencing films, inquire at the AFLA, 601 Curtis Street, Albany, California 94706.

Foil Fundamentals. 16mm black and white film with interspersed descriptive titles by George Santelli. Excellent film presentation of opening salute, on guard, foot movements, attacks, and parries. Available by purchase or rental from the AFLA, 33 62nd Street, West New York, N.J. 07093.

Let's Take a Trip. 16mm black and white sound film originally prepared by television personality Sonny Fox. Outstanding film for public information made at the Fencers Club in New York City. Fine presentation of foil, épée, and saber fencing and practice bouts. Available by rental from the AFLA, 33 62nd Street, West New York, N.J. 07093.

Modern Fundamentals of Foil Fencing. Portfolio of 16 illustrations covering basic positions, attacks, and parries. 11″ × 14″ black and white, photographed by

A. John Geraci. Also in 35mm projection slides. Available by purchase from Mr. Geraci, 279 East Northfield Road, Livingston, N.J. 07039.

NCAA 1980 Foil-Saber-Epée Finals (held at The Pennsylvania State University). ½" or ¾" color videotape originally prepared by ESPN cable television company of Bristol, Connecticut, for national television presentation in March 1980. Outstanding performances of national college finalists, with descriptive interpretation of actions and rules. A fine educational documentary. Available for rental from The Pennsylvania State University, c/o Maxwell R. Garret, 267 Recreation Building, University Park, Pennsylvania 16802.

Omnibus. 16mm black and white sound film originally prepared by the Ford Foundation for television. Outstanding film for general audience presentation to arouse interest in fencing. Excellent cinematography. Available from AFLA, 33 62nd Street, West New York, N.J. 07093.

Techniques of Foil Fencing. 16mm black and white film featuring Helene Mayer, former world champion, in a presentation of fencing positions and actions in normal and slow motion with close-ups of hand and foot movements on offense and defense. Available by purchase or rental from the University of California, Extension Film Center, 2223 Fulton Street, Berkeley, California 94720.

Glossary and Index of Fencing Terms

Note: Page numbers are in parentheses.

Absence of blades. The situation in which the opponents' blades are not in contact. (25)

Advance. A forward movement of the body executed by moving the leading foot first and following with the rear foot (without crossing them). The opposite of *retreat.* (17, 18, 27)

AFLA. Amateur Fencers League of America. (10, 91, 113)

Aids (fingers). The last three fingers (middle, ring, small) of the weapon hand. Compare *manipulators.* (13, 26, 30)

Attack. A simple or compound aggressive action to score. (32, 33, 43)

Attention position. The fencer stands erect with feet at right angles as in the diagram on page 14. The weapon arm is extended with the foil pointed diagonally downward and forward and with the point just slightly off the floor. The mask is cradled by the rear arm with the meshwork facing forward. (13)

Balestra. A method of attack that employs a jump forward with the lunge. (49)

Barrage. A fence-off due to a tie. (62, 63, 64)

Beat. A sharp, controlled blow against the middle or weak part of the opponent's blade to open a line of attack or to provoke a reaction. (27, 30, 31)

Beat attack. An attack in which the fencer's weapon strikes the opponent's blade to deflect it before launching the final offensive movement. (30, 31)

Bell guard. The metallic part of the weapon, circular and convex, that protects the hand. Also known as the *coquille.* (3, 7, 8, 9, 16, 23, 24, 79, 80)

Bind. Taking of the blade from high line to low line or vice versa. Compare *croisé.* (46)

Blade. A foil blade is made of flexible steel. Its cross section is quadrangular and its maximum length forward of the bell guard is 90 centimeters. (3, 7, 9, 80)

Body cord. The electrical wiring cord worn by the fencer which connects the weapon to the electrical apparatus. (76, 79, 80, 81)

Bout. The formal personal combat between two fencers; see *fencing bout.* To engage in a bout. (37, 38)

Button. The extremity of the blade, flat at the tip of the foil. In the electric foil, the button (tip) is called the *point.* (8)

Cadence. A fencing rhythm. (54)

Change beat. A beat executed by a change of engagement. (30, 31)

Change of engagement. The act of engaging in a new line. (26, 27)

Close. To cover a line of engagement (by the defender's weapon) against a straight thrust. (28)

Closed line. Refers to a line of engagement when the defender's weapon has covered or closed the line to a straight thrust. (28)

Coulé. The French term for a *glide,* which is a thrust in the line of engagement while keeping contact with the opponent's blade. (31, 32)

Counter-time actions. Movements of second intention. (47)

Coupé attack. The French term for *cutover*. (44)

Croisé. A blade-taking action that carries the opposing weapon from a high line to a low line, but on the same side as the engagement, not diagonally across the body as with the bind. (46, 47)

Cuissard. The portion of a fencing jacket that protects the groin area. (10)

Cutover. A form of disengage that passes over the point of the opposing blade. (33)

Deceive of the blade. An action that consists of removing one's blade from an opponent's attempt to make contact with it. (30, 32)

Deceive of the parry. An offensive action consisting of avoiding the opponent's attempt to block the attacking blade or make contact with it. (30, 32)

Direct thrust-cutover attack. A direct thrust is a feint delivered in the line of engagement, followed by the cutover as the final action of the attack. (44)

Disengage. A movement in which the blade passes from one line of engagement into another line. (26)

Disengagement. A simple attack, or riposte, which consists of leaving the line of engagement to go into the opposite line. (26)

Distance. See *fencing distance.*

Doublé attack. A compound attack commenced by a disengage feint and a deceive of the circular parry. (44)

Engagement of blades. A crossing of the blades and making contact. (25, 26, 28)

Envelopment. A taking of the opponent's blade which, by describing a circle with both blades in contact, returns to the line of engagement. (47)

Escrime. The French term for *fencing.* (91, 104)

Extension. A thrusting action of the weapon arm. (18, 19, 30)

Feint. An offensive movement made to resemble an attack or the beginning of an attack. Its aim is to draw a reaction or parry. (30)

Fencing bout. A contest between two adversaries. To win, a fencer must score five touches on the opponent within six minutes of *actual* fencing time. (4)

Fencing distance. The space between two fencers at any given time. (17, 18, 33, 34, 54)

Fencing master. A teacher or coach who has been accredited and licensed to instruct in three weapons—foil, saber, and épée. (104, 105)

Fencing measure. The distance between two fencers which requires extending the weapon arm and lunging in order to touch the opponent. (33, 34)

Fencing tempo. Basically, the amount of time required to execute one simple fencing action. (47, 65)

FIE. Fédération Internationale d'Escrime (International Fencing Federation). (91)

Flèche attack. An attack in which the fencer's body is propelled forward by a leaping-running action that normally causes the fencer to pass the opponent. (48, 49)

Foible. The one-third part of the blade nearest the tip. (7, 8)

Forte. The one-third part of the blade nearest the bell guard. (7, 8)

Froissement. An attack on the opponent's blade with a strong, sharp, accentuated glide along the blade to deflect it. (32)

Glide. A thrust in the line of engagement while keeping contact with the opponent's blade. Also called a *graze*. The French term is *coulé*. (30, 31, 32)

Graze. See *glide*. (4, 32)

Grip. The manner in which the weapon is held. (8)

Guard. See *bell guard*.

Handle. The part (of wood, metal, or plastic) by which the weapon is held. (7, 8, 9, 16)

High-low attack. The first action is a feint in the high line to draw the parry. The second action is avoiding the parry and moving the blade into the low line. (44)

Hilt. A portion of the weapon composed of three parts: the bell guard, the handle, and the pommel. (8)

Instructor. A teacher or coach who has been accredited and licensed to instruct in at least one weapon. (104, 105)

Judge. The individual who determines materiality of a hit. (37, 59, 60, 65)

Lamé. Metallic cloth designed to meet valid target specifications of the fencer for electric foil fencing. (76, 79, 81)

Leading. For a right-handed fencer, *leading* refers to the right hand and/or right leg. For a left-handed fencer, *leading* refers to the left hand and/or left leg. (14, 16, 17, 18, 19, 20, 27, 32)

Liability. A responsibility between parties which the courts recognize and enforce. *Waiver* of liability is the affirmative, intentional relinquishment of any claim for redress for injuries caused by another party's negligence. (108, 109)

Liability insurance. Personal insurance policies against liability can be carried with private companies or with professional and service organizations. The carrier assumes financial responsibility. (108)

Line (fencing line). A term dividing the areas of attack and defense—inside, outside, high, low—related to the position of the hand and the weapon. (23, 24, 41, 42)

Low-high attack. The first action is a feint into the low line to draw the parry. The second action is avoiding the parry and moving the blade into the high line. (44)

Lunge. A forward movement executed by advancing the leading foot toward the opponent while the rear foot remains stationary (usually following the extension of the weapon arm). (19, 20)

Manipulators (fingers). The index finger and thumb of the hand holding the weapon. (13)

Martingale. An attachment anchored inside the bell guard, which can be looped around the weapon hand. When the foil is not secured to the hand by a body wire, a martingale is mandatory. (9)

Master. See *fencing master*.

Measure. See *fencing measure*.

NFCAA. National Fencing Coaches Association of America. (91)

Octave. The position that covers (protects) the low outside line. The hand is supinated, with the point lower than the hand. (24, 42)

On deck. The next two scheduled adversaries are required to be "on deck" and
ready to compete when the bout in progress is completed. (66)

On guard. The fundamental position of the fencer preparing to bout with his
opponent. (13, 15, 16, 17, 37)

One-two attack. This attack involves two disengages. The first disengage is a feint
designed to draw a direct (lateral) parry, and the second disengage is a
deceive of the intended parry. (43)

Open line(s). Area(s) or position(s) unprotected. When a line is opened voluntarily,
the action becomes an invitation to attack. (24)

Opposition. A movement of taking and not releasing the opponent's blade. (47)

Orthopedic handle. An idiomatic term applied to molded handles. (9)

Overload principle. A gradual progressive increase of resistance that will tend to
strengthen muscles, enabling them to react with greater force. (69, 70)

Pad. A cushion or padding located inside the bell guard to absorb shocks. (7, 8)

Parry. A defensive action made with the weapon to deflect the attacker's blade. To
take such action. (27, 28, 29, 30)

Phrase. An uninterrupted exchange of blade actions, ending either with a touch or
with the fencers breaking off the action. Also known as *phrase d'armes.* (38,
59, 60)

Piste. The strip or mat. (4, 37, 79)

Pistol handle. See *orthopedic handle.*

Plastron. A protective undergarment for the weapon armpit and side. (10)

Point control. The correct execution of blade movements, by keeping the point in
line to threaten the opponent's target. (19)

Pommel. A metal piece at the extreme rear of the handle, which serves the dual
purpose of locking together the different parts of the weapon and acting as a
counterweight to the blade. (7, 9, 16, 80)

Pool. A tournament term for several fencers assigned to compete against each
other. (61–64)

President. The arbitrator or director of the bout. (37, 59, 60, 61, 64, 65, 86)

Pressure. A lateral blade press upon the opponent's blade. (30, 32)

Prevost. A preliminary status of an accredited and licensed fencing teacher or
coach before achieving the Master certificate. See *fencing master.* (104,
105)

Prime. A position that protects (covers) the low inside area, thumb toward six
o'clock, hand in pronation, with the point lower than the hand. (24)

Pronation. The position of the weapon hand with the fingernails and palm down.
(24)

Quarte. A position that covers (protects) the inside high area. The point is higher
than the hand, which is in supination. (24)

Quinte. A position that covers (protects) the inside high area. The point is higher than the hand, which is in pronation. (24)

Rear (vs. leading). For a right-handed fencer, *rear* refers to the left hand and/or left leg. For a left-handed fencer, *rear* refers to the right hand and/or right leg. (14, 16, 18, 19, 20, 27)

Recover (recovery). Return to the on-guard position. (23)

Redoublement. A new indirect attack made against an opponent who has failed to riposte. (45, 46)

Remise. An immediate direct offensive action by the attacker, without withdrawal of the weapon arm, against an opponent who has failed to immediately riposte, made in the same line. (45, 46)

Reprise. An action where the opponent fails to immediately riposte and the attacker renews the offensive. (45)

Retreat. To step back, moving the rear foot first and then the lead foot (without crossing them). The opposite of *advance.* (17, 18, 27)

Ricasso. On an Italian foil, the flattened part of the blade's tang within the bell guard, between the bell guard and the cross bar. (8)

Right of way. A conventional rule of play for foil and saber. (29, 49)

Riposte. The offensive action which follows a successful parry. (28, 29)

Salute. Formal acknowledgment, executed with the weapon, to the opponent, officials, and spectators. (13, 14)

Scorekeeper. One who maintains the on-going record of a bout. (37, 59, 61, 66, 86, 87)

Second intention. A premeditated action with a provoked movement. (47)

Seconde. A position that covers (protects) the inside low area, taken with the point lower than the hand, which is in pronation. (24)

Semicircular parry. A parry that describes a half circle from high to low line, or vice versa. (42, 43, 44)

Septime. A position that covers (protects) the inside low area, with the point lower than the hand, which is in supination. (24, 42)

Sixte. A position that covers (protects) the outside high area; taken with the point higher than the hand, which is supinated. The on-guard position in sixte is traditional. (24)

Steal (the time). To take an action that will touch the opponent's target before the opponent's final movement of the attack arrives. (47)

Stop hit. A counteroffensive action which, to be valid, must land before the attacker's final movement. (47, 48)

Straight thrust. A simple, direct attack. (32)

Supination. The position of the weapon hand with the fingernails and palm up. (16, 18, 24, 26, 28)

Taking the (opponent's) blade. A preparation for attack, also called *prise de fer.* (46)

Tempo. See *fencing tempo.*

Thrust. Extension of the weapon arm. (18)

Tierce. A position that covers (protects) the outside high area, taken with the hand in pronation and with the point higher than the hand. (24)

Time action. A stop hit executed by closing the line in which the attack is to be completed. (47)

Timekeeper. One who controls the stopwatch during a bout. (37, 59, 61, 66, 87)

Timing. Basically, seizing one's opportunity and executing an attack at the precise instant in which to take an opponent by surprise. (34)

USAA. United States Academy of Arms. (91)

Valid hit. A touch scored within the prescribed target area with the point of the weapon. (4, 81, 82)